MASTERS RACEWALKING

MASTERS RACEWALKING

American Coaches and Athletes Share Ideas on Technique, Training and Racing

EDITED BY ELAINE P. WARD

N.A.R.F. Publishing, Pasadena, CA

Masters Racewalking
American Coaches and Athletes
Share Ideas on Technique, Training and Racing

Published by:
N.A.R.F. Publishing
Post Office Box 50312
Pasadena, CA 91115-0312
Tel/Fax: 818-577-2264

First Printing 1996

Publisher's Cataloging in Publication
(Prepared by Quality Books Inc.)

Ward, Elaine P.
Masters racewalking: American coaches and athletes share ideas on technique, training and racing / Elaine P. Ward.
p. cm.
Preassigned LCCN: 95-71241.
ISBN: 1-884647-03-0.

1. Walking (Sports) I. Title.

GV1071.W37 1996 796.42'9
QBI95-20634

DEDICATION

This book celebrates the Masters Racewalking Community and its unique camaraderie and dedication. Throughout America, masters are quietly providing the support, ideas and positive leadership needed to make racewalking a fully recognized alternative for athletes of all ages.

AMERICAN RACEWALKING FOUNDATION

P.O. BOX 50312, PASADENA, CA 91115-0312
TEL/FAX: 818-577-2264
E-mail: NARWF@aol.com

The North American Racewalking Foundation has the purpose of promoting racewalking throughout the United States. We provide information about racewalking clubs, coaches and camps. When there are no immediate contacts available, the Foundation provides video coaching and training programs for beginning and intermediate athletes. We also market books and videos on racewalking by several authors.

The Foundation has a growing membership with extensive membership benefits. Over the years, we have funded youth programs and recently established a Masters Competition Fund for tax deductible donations to help masters athletes go to important national and international competitions. Wherever there appears to be a need, we make an effort to supply a solution.

For further information about the Foundation's services and resources, write to Elaine Ward, N.A.R.F., P.O. Box 50312, Pasadena, CA 91115-0312. Phone/Fax: 818-577-2264. E-mail: NARWF@aol.com

TABLE OF CONTENTS

MASTERS MEN ATHLETES

GOVERNING BODIES, PROCEDURES, RULES

Dear Reader,

The knowledge and experiences of coaches and athletes are timeless. The years may bring alterations in technique or in the rules of a sport, but athletic experience holds true. *MASTERS RACEWALKING* explores the mental and physical preparation and competitive challenges of men and women racewalkers between the years 1990 and 1995.

Some of the material in this book was first presented as interviews in "The Southern California Racewalking News" and later in "National Masters News." Some material is original to this book. It is important to emphasize that many fine athletes and coaches are not included here only because our paths did not meet when I had a tape recorder in hand.

I would particularly like to call attention to the final section, "Governing Bodies, Procedures and Rules." Bev LaVeck and Bob Fine have provided extensive information on masters Age Graded Tables, awards, records, and championships as well as on the administrative hierarchy of WAVA, IAAF and USATF. All this information has been updated and is being presented in one convenient place for the first time.

It is the hope of all who contributed to this book that novice and elite racewalkers alike will find it a continuing and helpful resource. Undoubtedly there are issues that are not covered. If you notice some omissions or have ideas and experiences that you feel are of universal interest, please write. They may well become the source material for a follow-up book.

Elaine Ward

Elaine Ward
North American Racewalking Foundation
P.O. Box 50312, Pasadena, CA 91115-0312.

PROLOGUE

LARRY WALKER

The following is an address made by Larry Walker at the banquet for the Youth Road Championships in Southern California, June 1988. Larry was a member of the 1976 and 1980 US Olympic Teams. In 1983, he began competing in the masters division and in the next years established over 40 Best Performances. Some of his fastest times were made at age 40: 1 mile 6:07; 2 mile 13:05; 5km 20:51; 10km 43:21. His best 20km is 1:32:05.

"My Personal Road to the Olympics" captures the indomitable spirit of the true competitor and provides insight and inspiration for racewalkers of any age on a personal quest for athletic success.

MY PERSONAL ROAD TO THE OLYMPICS

I am probably the most improbable person that I can imagine to have made an Olympic team. In grade school I was the last one to get picked for any team. I was a perennial bench warmer and carry a great number of splinters even today from that experience.

When I finally got a chance to compete, it was in baseball. I was always put in right field where the birdies sing because they figured that was the most harmless place to put me. For a while in high school it looked like things weren't getting any better.

Finally, I had some athletic success my first year in track. I could not do anything very coordinated, but I could do it a long time. My coach told a friend of mine on the sly, "Walker runs like an elephant." Well, that was not very flattering. And when the Athletic Banquet came around, my coach dug deep for something nice to say about me and came up with, "Well, Larry Walker doesn't have any talent, but he tries hard."

That was something of a rather minor, crushing defeat, but I went on and continued to compete through college and eventually got into racewalking. Then came 1976. I decided if I was going to have a chance to compete in the Olympics, this was the year. When the day of the Olympic Trials came, I had no idea how fast my competitors walked. Even to this day I studiously avoid reading anything outside the *Southern California Racewalking News.* So as we lined up at the start, I heard that I was 18th fastest in the field of 21 walkers.

Too late to panic. The gun went off and 42 legs and 42 lungs went heaving forward. The first few miles felt pretty decent. Then all of a sudden fatigue started hitting and I started cramping. I tried to hold on, but the guys were getting farther ahead. I thought about it being my last chance and kept trying, but nothing was working. It really felt bad seeing my chance slipping away.

Then I started drinking ERG and started feeling better. At about eight miles, I passed Tom Dooley who had already been on an Olympic Team and I thought, "Son of a gun." Then I went a little farther and with two or three miles to go, I could see the three leaders ahead. I thought, "Wow, this is fantastic. I might not make it, but this is not shabby." With one lap or about one mile to go, I moved by Larry Young. He already had two bronze medals so I figured he did not need any more. I opened up about 45 seconds in the last mile, and all of a sudden, my thoughts were on making the team.

When Martin Rudow started shouting from a flat bed truck, "Here is your Olympic team — Tod Scully, Ron Laird and Larry Walker," it really sank in. The three of us entered the stadium and about 20,000 people were making a lot of noise. Fortunately, I stayed on the ground, but I felt like I was five feet off. I finished the race, saw Tod and grabbed his arm. We laughed and cried. I have no idea what we said. All I remember was saying to him that just before the race about the last thing I did was to go up to the chapel and appeal to a higher authority. Scully said that he had done something similar.

Of my Olympic experience I want to tell you a couple of things about the people I met. All the stereotypes which come from the media accentuate the negative. If someone is caught on drugs, it is splashed on the headlines. The 99 percent who are clean and working hard don't get any publicity. But,

I observed two things that are solidly true in my fellow athletes.

First, they are vastly more intelligent than they are given credit for. Probably not more than one or two people in this room are aware that Edwin Moses graduated from Morehouse College with nearly straight A's in physics and math. We had two doctors, one lawyer and an engineer on the '76 Olympic team. There were more advanced degrees than you can shake a stick at, but who knows this? I think it should be known.

The second thing I found was a depth of religious feeling among the athletes I met. I walked with Mormons, Baptists, Catholics and others, and found that wherever I went there was much more depth than I was ever led to believe from the accounts in the newspapers.

These observations bring me to the last point: What is being an athlete all about? For any of you who have ever gone to the top of a mountain during a workout and looked miles down to the start point, or who have ever been in a race when it was just a pure, clear, beautiful, perfect day — you know the great feeling. But this is not what makes someone an athlete. It is going out when it is too hot, too cold, too windy, too rainy, or when your muscles are aching and guts bursting. You feel miserable, but you still put on your track shorts and go out and do it. This is what makes an athlete. It does not matter how old you are. It is the day to day training.

Again, what is being an athlete all about? I believe that our talent is God's gift to us. In the striving, in the racing, in the losing and the winning, in the so-called agony of defeat, we somehow dedicate ourselves through our athletics back to the source of our talent so that our sport has meaning and ultimately our life has meaning.

COACHES

FRANK ALONGI

BOHDAN BULAKOWSKI

GWEN ROBERTSON

MIKE DEWITT

MARTIN RUDOW

Frank Alongi

L to R: Paul Johnson, Bohdan Bulakowski, Bill Barnes

COACH FRANK ALONGI

The most important principle for an older walker is not to try to do what younger athletes do.

A good training program is like the athlete's Bible as it brings him or her to higher and higher levels of performance.

I Italian Heritage
II Coaching
III Training
IV Technique with Elaine Ward

In September of each year, Frank Alongi and The Wolverine Pacers host the Alongi International Racewalk Classic (formerly known as the Casimiro Alongi Memorial International Racewalk). Since the race's inception in 1979, the men's 20km race has been won by such international greats as Carlo Mattioli, Giovanni Perricelli and Maurizio Damilano from Italy; Bernardo Segura, Ernesto Canto and Raul Gonzalez from Mexico; Tim Barrett from Great Britain (now Canada); Guillaume Leblanc from Canada, Zbigniew Sadlej from Poland; and Tim Lewis and Carl Schueler from the United States. The women's 10km has been won by Ileana Salvador from Italy, Graciela Mendoza and Francisca Martinez from Mexico, Anne Peel from Canada, and Debbi Lawrence and Theresa Vaill from the United States of America.

Frank's story is one firmly based on old world discipline, natural talent and dedicated love of sport. His background provides an essential key to understanding his coaching philosophy. His vision of athletic excellence is that of the young boy who became an Olympian in a war torn environment of devastation and poverty. Though he modifies his training programs according to the age and abilities of his masters athletes, his principles of consistent and progressive hard work are the same for all ages.

ITALIAN HERITAGE

Frank was born in Palermo, Italy before World War II. He is the oldest of eleven children. The following is his life story as he tells it.

I became a track man by accident. I was training for soccer, but one day my professor of physical education in high school said to me, "Franco, we have the city championship coming. Can you compete in the cross-country event? Even if you finish last, you will bring our team a point." He explained that the two best runners in my school were sick with influenza and said, "At least you will like being with all your buddies, and you can try to do the best that you can."

It was a 3km race and I agreed to run. At the start, I took off like lightening, just like I was running a 100 meter dash. I never looked back. It was a natural course. There was a water jump and a creek to pass. I finished in 9:57 and established a new state cross-country record.

I was only 16-years-old and they accused me of cheating. They said I cut the course. However, when they checked all the monitor's cards, their cards showed that I had gone through the whole course. Nonetheless, nobody believed my finish because the second place runner was 300 meters behind me. Generally, the second place runner is 2 meters, 10 meters, maybe 20 meters behind, but not 300 meters. Even my physical education instructor could not believe I had run so fast and asked me if I had cheated.

The first six runners from this 3km cross-country championship qualified for the state championships. Since Sicily had ten provinces, sixty people were in the finals. The finals were held in Messina and I did the same thing again. I won setting another new Italian record for cross-country. My time was 9:20. Now people started to believe.

NATIONAL CHAMPION

Four weeks later I had to compete in the National Championships in Montecatini, Tuscany. When I went there, the weather was cold. It was not like our part of Italy. Everybody in Tuscany had beautiful sweat suits. What I had was long-johns. My mother put two buttons in the front and that was it. All the other runners I saw had track shoes with cleats or spikes. I had an old pair of tennis shoes. The only track shoes I had ever seen was a pair we shared at school. You see, my school was not equipped. Our track had craters from being bombed. We filled them with charcoal, mixed some sand with water and rolled this mixture over the charcoal to make as flat a surface as possible. In spite of the poverty, I won the race in Tuscany and became the cross-country national champion.

Suddenly Franco Alongi became popular. People began talking about me. When I arrived home on the train, the whole town was at the depot. The butcher, who lived near my house said, "Franco, come over here." He picked up a steak. "Take home. Go to eat the steak. You need this. You are a little bit pale in your face. You need this." The fruit store owner, "Veni qui, Franco." He gave me apples and grapes to take home. Everyone was giving me things — coffee, pastry, so much.

The cross-country triumph was the inspiration for me to take physical education. I wanted to go back to my school and teach kids how to run, how to shot put, how to throw the discus and javelin. Though my long range goal was to become an engineer, I decided to go to Rome to become a physical education teacher. As I had maintained an A average in school, I was admitted to ISEF (Istituto Superiore Educazione Fisica) in Rome even though I could not pay.

The trip to Rome was unbelievable by today's standards. After the war, things were so bad that no train was able to run on time. It took me two days to travel to Rome. I slept in the luggage rack and existed on two loaves of bread, a piece of cheese and a jar of water. It was two days with soot and cinders from the engine flying into my eyes every time someone opened a window.

I was happy because I wanted to go to Rome, the capital of Italy. I did not know the difference between a small town and a big city. I discovered that Rome was not like my home town where I could walk everywhere. You had to go 10 to 15 miles to get from one place to the next. You had to take a train, a cab or a bicycle. Nothing was close. But I managed and spent three lovely years there. I became a member of the Fiat sports club because Fiat not only manufactured automobiles, but had one of the best track teams in the country.

1948 OLYMPICS

In 1948, I was invited to compete in the Olympic Trials. It was early May and I went to the stadium Le Terme de Caracalla, a stadium the

Romans used. At that time the track was cinder and I planned to compete in the 5000 meter event. Again, I just had my old tennis shoes and the right one had a big hole. I took a piece of fabric from an old suitcase and slipped it inside the shoe to cover the hole. It kept my foot from coming in contact with the track. No one wore socks in any track event then.

When the race started, I took off and lapped everybody. I was the youngest person to go below 15:00 in a 5km. By the end of the race, my right foot was bleeding so badly that I had one red shoe and one white shoe. I picked up a piece of lemon, squeezed it on the wound to disinfect it, picked out all of the cinders with my fingers and then tied a handkerchief around my foot for protection. That was the start of my career as a 5,000 meter and 10,000 meter runner. In 1948, I ran the 5,000 and 10,000 meter events in the Olympics.

In 1949, I graduated from ISEF and my thesis was a comparison of Olympic racewalking techniques. I had a 35mm movie and compared the styles of Frigerio, Altamani and Pavesi. They were the three greatest Italian walkers of that time. Making this comparison for my thesis was how I started racewalking.

In order to become an engineer, I enlisted in the Italian navy and became an underwater demolition expert. I officially came to America in September of 1956 and went to work for Chrysler. From 1961 to April 1964, I worked for NASA on the lunar rover vehicle. There was an explosion, a big disaster. My back was broken, I lost one eye and had 40 stitches across my head. But I still had my life. After that, I went to work for Ford and have been there ever since.

COACHING

Coaching is something special. It is something you learn from experience and something that requires daily innovation. You have to be constantly updating yourself because what you learned in the past may be dead wrong.

When I was young, a person had to work very, very hard to achieve a goal. Today, the finest athletes still work very, very hard, but there are also technical aids for training such as video cameras and high-speed photography. Physiologists are computerizing the biomechanics of runners, walkers, jumpers and throwers. These studies are providing coaches with models of the most efficient techniques for their athletes. Specifically, they provide racewalking coaches with a basic understanding of how to maximize the performances of their athletes.

No two athletes are alike. It is the responsibility of the coach to adapt biomechanically sound technique to each individual's particular build to get the greatest efficiency and speed. That is why coaching is difficult. It is necessary to know the body, mind and spirit of each athlete.

Sometimes you may have an athlete with a perfect body, but he does not have the right attitude. Some are temperamental and some are easy going. Some athletes have very fast reflexes and some have slow reflexes. Some are very coordinated and some are not. Some are strong and some are weak.

You also have to know such things as an athlete's eating habits. Maybe a particular individual cannot train after eating because he gets stomach cramps. It is best for him to train on an empty stomach. You will have another athlete who cannot train unless he has ten pounds of food inside his stomach. Then there is the individual who does not need any water during training while another will need a gallon of water every lap. You also have athletes who are great trainers, but lousy competitors

FOUR SIGNS

As a coach, you look for four signs in an athlete. First, you look for basic health. You cannot send everyone to a laboratory for a checkup, but you can see whether an athlete has good color or is pale; robust or fragile.

The second sign you look for is the impediments an individual has. Maybe one hip is a little lower than the other, or maybe there is some scoliosis of the spine. If an athlete has a handicap, it does not mean that he or she cannot be a superstar. Consider Maurizio Damilano. His right clavicle is 2 1/2 inches shorter than his left. Occasionally when you see him walk, you will see one shoulder start to droop and see him deliberately raise it.

The third sign is speed. If an individual has a leg speed less than 180 steps per minute, he or she can become a very good fitness walker, but not an elite athlete. If the individual has 200 steps per minute the potential is better; 210 steps is better yet. A coach can improve the speed of an athlete between 10 to 20 percent, but no more than that. Speed has to be part of the individual's genetic characteristics.

The fourth sign is attitude toward learning. Attitude is special. There are people who can be told something once and they will do it. There are others who have to be told many times. It does not matter. I have seen both fast learners and slow learners achieve phenomenal goals. Every coach hopes for fast learners. But the good coach excels when he can bring out the best in both types and build them into superstars.

Sometimes a disqualification helps a racewalker. The exuberance of speed makes him or her forget about technique. This is why the coach and the athlete have to be very close. The coach is the one who has to teach the athlete how to perform well. Do not blame the judge. If the athlete is doing something wrong, blame the coach.

AGE AS A FACTOR

The most important principle for an older walker is not to try to do what younger athletes do. Their pulse rates are not the same. Masters walkers are usually stiffer. It takes longer for them to get the racewalking technique into their body's movements. As a result they require longer supervision.

Max Green started racewalking after he was 50 and his success comes from his patience. He racewalks because he wants to, and he is always trying to do better. Even if his body does not respond the way he wants, he competes with all his heart. He is a winner because he never gives up. His persistence is the reason he has made such good times and accomplished his goals.

Besides being patient, it is **very important** for masters to do limbering and stretching exercises. This is especially so before workouts. If they do not, they will get injured. Once an older person is injured, it takes a long time to heal. This can be discouraging to some. It is easier to say, "I am old and might as well quit," than to say, "It's going to take time to heal, and I must be patient." Some older people feel they do not have much time left and they feel impatient.

Another must for the older walker is to train consistently. A younger person may be able to lay off training a few days, come back and have a good race. An older person cannot. Masters who are seriously competitive need to train consistently to maintain their conditioning. They must have a strong desire.

BODY TYPES

In determining which body types are best for racewalking, you need to consider an athlete's height, weight and morphology.

Athletes can be divided into three height groups:

Tall:	180 cm (71 inches) and above
Medium:	170 to 180 cm (67-71 inches)
Short:	Less than 170 cm (67 inches)

The three weight groups: The RYBAKOV formula selects the body weight in relation to the K factor of each athlete.

K = (h -100)/w. h = height (cm) w = weight (kg)

Conversion: 1 cm =.39 inch; 1 kg = 2.2046 pounds.

Heavy:	K = 0.95 or below
Medium:	K = 0.95 to 1.005
Light:	K = 1.005 and above

Examples: h = 180 cm & w = 100 kg K = 0.80 - Heavy
& w = 80 kg K = 1.00 - Medium
& w = 70 kg K = 1.142 Light

The three major morphologic types are:

Brachial (long arms)
Normal
Longen (long muscles)

From the 27 athletic categories, racewalkers usually fall into the following groups:

Muscle Type	Body Type	Body Weight
Longen	Short	Light
Longen	Medium	Light
Longen	Tall	Light
Normal	Short	Light
Normal	Medium	Light
Normal	Tall	Light

TRAINING

Training schedules are the work of a programmer. In most countries, the programmer is the person who decides what the individual athlete does. The coach is the individual who makes the athlete understand the training program and sees that the athlete follows it. A good training program is like the athlete's Bible as it brings him or her to higher and higher levels of performance.

As the human being is changeable, it is necessary to set up a program that builds a solid base. If the base is broad, it is possible to build a super athlete. If the base is narrow, the athlete is fragile and may pull a muscle or get a stress fracture. A broad base prevents injury and provides the endurance for maintaining speed.

HEART RATE

Much has been written about using the heart rate as a training tool. If you train an athlete to handle a certain work load at a certain heart rate, that athlete can go for hours without anything bothering him or her as long as there is enough fuel for energy. The moment the blood sugar goes down, the heart rate and body temperature go up, and the athlete is unable to compete further.

To make a training schedule for an athlete, it is necessary to test his or her heart rate. To do this testing, you need a heart rate monitor, a stop watch and a measured course like a track. You want to be able to record the athlete's pulse rate, speed and distance walked.

Before testing the athlete should warm up very well to stabilize the pulse rate. During testing the athlete walks laps at an ever quickening pace per minute; i.e. 150, 160, 170, 180, 190, 200 paces, or any appropriate progression depending on age. When a lap is completed, the pulse rate is recorded. At a certain point, the upward curve of the pulse line flattens out. The walker is beginning to lose oxygen from the blood as well as beginning to build up lactic acid. Essentially, he or she is becoming anaerobic. This point is the ledge point.

A person once asked me why the curve goes flat. It flattens because the heart is a pump and at some point, it cannot pump harder or faster. When the curve flattens out, the heart is saying, "I have had enough."

If a walker has a problem heart and trains above his or her ledge point, the risk of serious disability is high. On the other hand, if athletes train just below their ledge points, they can maximize the benefits of their training without injury. Using the pulse rate is a good way to avoid the excesses that lead to physical distress and injury. The following are examples of workouts that can be adjusted to the age and condition of a walker.

ANAEROBIC THRESHOLD TEST

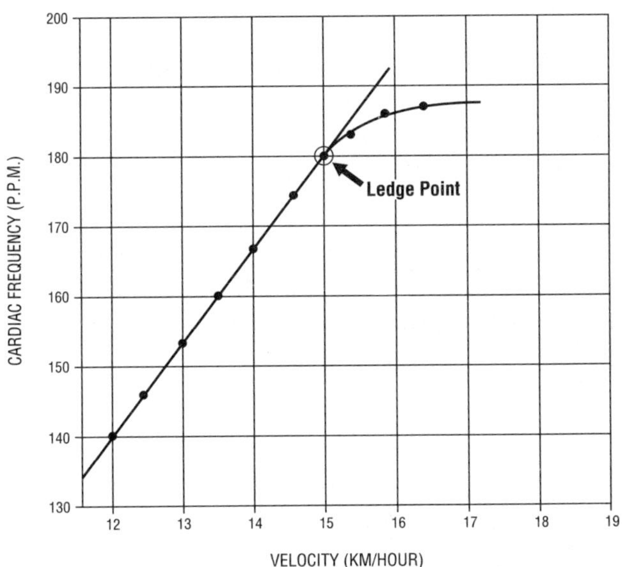

ANAEROBIC POWER TRAINING METHOD

1. STEADY PACE AT HIGH SPEED
2. INTERVALS
3. HILLS

MASTERS WOMEN Examples of three types of anaerobic threshold (A.T.) workouts, masters women training for a 10 km.

1. 5 km to 6 km @ 5% to 8% below A. T.
2. 5 km to 7 km @ 3% below A.T. Intervals of 1 km.
3. 3 km to 5 km repeats of 200 to 500 meter hills @ 5% to 7% below A.T.

MASTERS MEN The following are examples of the three types of anaerobic workouts for masters men training for a 20 Km.

1. 8 km to 12 km @ 5% to 8% below A.T.
2. 10 km to 15 km @ 3% below A.T. Intervals of 1 km to 3 km.
3. 6 km to 10 km of repeats of 200 to 500 meter hill climb @ 5% to 7% below A.T.

Do anaerobic training according to your age, conditioning and training needs. Speed is properly based on your ledge point or anaerobic threshold. Every training program must be individual.

AEROBIC POWER TRAINING METHODS

1. LONG DISTANCE
2. SLOW WALKING
3. MEDIUM SPEED
4. COMPETITION SPEED
5. VARIABLE SPEED

MASTERS WOMEN The following are examples of the five types of aerobic workouts for masters women training for 10 Km.

1. 12 km to 15 km @ 18% to 20% below A.T.
2. 10 km to 12 km @ 15% to 18% below A.T.
3. 8 km to 10 km @ 15% below A.T.
4. 6 km to 8 km @ 10% to 12% below A.T., or
   3 to 4 repeats of 2 km 10% below A.T.
5. 5 km to 7.5 km changing speeds between
   20%—10% below A.T. using 1 km to 2 km intervals.

MASTERS MEN The following are examples of the five types of aerobic workouts for masters men training for 20 Km.

1. 25 km to 30 km @ 18% to 20% below A.T.
2. 15 km to 20 km @ 15% to 18% below A.T.
3. 10 km to 15 km @ 15% below A.T.
4. 8 km to 12 km @ 10% to 12% below A.T., or
   4 to 5 repeats of 2 km 10% below A.T.
5. 9 km to 10 km changing speed between
   20% below A.T. for 3 km and 10% for 2 km

Again, do aerobic workouts according to your age, conditioning and overall training needs. The distances should be adjusted for your individual goals. Speeds are properly related to your anaerobic threshold. A heart rate monitor can be helpful.

A REGULAR TRAINING PROGRAM This workout program is designed for a man, age 49, Anaerobic Threshold 178 PPM @ 5:00. Projection: 46:40 10 km or 1:35:00 20 km. No. 6 stands for 6 consecutive workouts at the given distance, followed by 5 workouts, etc.

Number	Distance	Program
6	25 km	20 km @ 5:40 + 5 km @ 5:30
5	25 km	20 km @ 5:35 + 5 km @ 5:30
4	25 km	15 km @ 5:35 + 10 km @ 5:30
3	25 km	15 km @ 5:30 + 10 km @ 5:20
6	17 km	10 km @ 5:20 + 7 km @ 5:10
5	17 km	14 km @ 5:20 + 2 km @ 5:10 + 1 km @ 5:00
4	17 km	14 km @ 5:10 + 2 km @ 5:00 + 1 km @ 4:50
3	17 km	14 km @ 5:10 + 2 km @ 5:00 + 1 km @ 4:40
5	25 km	10 km @ 5:20 + 10 km @ 5:10 + 5 km @ 5:00
4	25 km	15 km @ 5:20 + 5 km @ 5:10 + 5 km @ 5:00
3	25 km	15 km @ 5:20 + 10 km @ 5:10
2	25 km	15 Km @ 5:20 + 5 km @ 5:10 + 5 km @ 5:00
5	17 km	10 km @ 5:20 + 7 km @ 5:00
4	17 km	10 km @ 5:10 + 7 km @ 5:00
5	17 km	10 km @ 5:10 + 4 km @ 5:00 + 3 km @ 4:50
4	17 km	8 km @ 5:10 + 5 km @ 5:00 + 4 km @ 4:50
5	17 km	7 km @ 5:10 + 6 km @ 5:00 + 4 km @ 4:50

4	25 km	5x5 km @ 5:10 (4:00 rest)
3	25 km	2x10 km @ 5:10 + 5 km @ 5:00 (7:00 rest)
4	25 km	5x5 km @ 5:00 (4:00 rest)
5	10 km	5x2 km @ 4:50 (3:00 rest)
4	10 km	10x1 km @ 4:50 (2:00 rest)

After this program, athlete should be reevaluated.

ALONGI RACEWALKING TECHNIQUE

During the 1970s, when racewalking was described as a "pulling" motion, Frank Alongi championed a new technique. He promoted walking with a forward lean to utilize gravity as runners do as well as walking with a continuous rolling/pushing motion from heel to toe. These ideas are now widely accepted. With a thorough understanding of biomechanics, Frank also introduced a number of exercises and stretches to facilitate learning the racewalking technique. You can find an adaptation of the Alongi Technique in the books, *Introduction to the Technique of Racewalking* and *Mobility Exercises for Racewalking* and the video, *The Basic Technique of Racewalking* by Elaine Ward and the Southern Cal Walkers. (See Appendix.) The following is written by Elaine Ward.

POSTURE: Body posture is essential to your racewalking technique. Correct posture has a forward lean from the ankles. The spine is straight. The buttocks and stomach are tucked in. The abdomen is firm. Shoulders are relaxed. Ears, shoulders, hips and ankles are in alignment.

FOOTWORK: As your leg swings forward, dorsiflex your foot raising your toes in a 35 to 45 degree angle with the ground. Proper heel contact is under your hip at your hip's most forward point of rotation. Keep your feet pointed forward.

After heel contact, roll forward on the fleshy outer part of the bottom of your foot. As your foot passes under your body, start pressing and pushing the ground with your forefoot until toe off. The gait is a continuous, smooth roll-push.

After toe off, keep your heel close to the ground as you bring your leg forward and dorsiflex your foot just before heel contact. Do not let the front of your foot slap down to the ground after heel contact. Do not walk flatfooted. Keep a smooth heel-to-toe roll and push.

STRAIGHT LEG: When you raise your toes just prior to heel contact, straighten your knee fully so that it is straight at heel contact and remains straight into the upright, support position. A straight leg in the support position acts as a firm lever for transferring the power accumulated in the front rolling phase of the footwork to the back pushing phase.

HIPS: Hip movement serves to increase stride length. The primary movement is a front-back rotation. There is slight up-down and lateral action as your weight transfers from leg to leg. This movement is often referred to as the "hip drop." There is no waddle, no sashay, or other wasteful sideways movement .

ARMS: The arms are bent at the elbows in an 85 degree angle. They are held close to the body and swing from relaxed shoulders. The swing line is at the level of your elbow when your arm is bent. This may be above your waist, at your waist or below your waist depending on the length of your arm from shoulder to elbow. In the forward swing, your elbow comes just beyond the center of your side, and in the backward swing, your wrist goes just behind your buttocks.

The range of your arm swing affects your stride length. If you take a short arm swing, your stride will be short. If you take a fuller swing, your stride will lengthen. The speed of your arms affects your leg turnover. The faster your arms move, the faster your legs turnover. The movements of the upper body and lower body properly mirror each other.

HANDS: Hold your hand in a loose fist with your thumb resting on your curled index finger. If you point your thumbs forward, you can monitor whether your arms are swinging back and forth at your sides or straying across your body.

HEAD: Keep your head up and eyes forward. If you are inclined to bend your head and look at the ground, keep in mind that you can see irregularities on the ground by lowering your eyes. If you walk with your head out of alignment, you create tension in your neck and shoulder muscles

It is good racewalking strategy to make a technique check as you are training and racing. Essentially, you carry on a question and answer dialogue with yourself.

INVENTORY TAKING

POSTURE..

1. Is my posture forward? Am I using gravity?
2. Is my spine straight?
3. Are my ears, shoulders, hips and ankles in alignment?
4. Are my shoulders relaxed?
5. Are my abdominal and buttocks muscles tucked in?
6. Is there a lift from my abdomen to my solar plexus?
7. Is my head up?

FOOTWORK..

1. At ground contact, is my heel aligned with the fleshy outer part of my foot?
2. Is heel contact under my hip?
3. Are my feet pointed forward as I roll forward?
4. Am I rolling from heel to toe in a smooth, unbroken motion?
5. Am I pushing the ground "back" with my forefoot and the pads of my toes?

LEGS..

1. Is my leg straight from heel contact into the upright support position?
2. Do I feel my ankle flexing and my forefoot raising?
3. Do I feel my calf muscles & Achilles tendon stretch with dorsiflexion of the foot?
4. Is my stride shorter in front than in back?

HIPS..

1. Am I moving my hips back and forth symmetrically?
2. Are my hips anticipating the forward movement of my legs so heel contact has minimum impact?
3. Am I completing my front/back hip rotation?
4. Can I feel my hips "drop" as my weight transfers in leg to leg as I'm walking?

TORSO..

1. Do I feel a twisting in my waistline from my oppositional arm and hip action?
2. Am I holding my abdominal muscles in (abs in) and tucking my buttocks under my body (glutes in)?
3. Do the muscles of my torso feel relaxed and limber?

ARMS..

1. Do I feel my wrists and elbows swinging close to my body?
2. Is my elbow remaining bent at an 85 degree angle?
3. Does my elbow stop just infront of the center of my body during the forward swing?
4. Does my wrist extend just behind my buttocks during the backward swing?
5. Are my thumbs resting lightly on my index fingers and pointing forward?
6. Is my back swing full and aiding my forward posture?

SHOULDERS..

1. Are my shoulders relaxed and down?
2. Are my arms swinging back and forth without causing any forward, inward roll to the shoulders?

NECK AND HEAD..

1. Is my neck relaxed and my head in alignment with my spine?
2. Is my chin up and eyes focused 20 to 30 feet in front of me?

RACEWALKING UPHILL AND DOWNHILL

Two of the most frequently asked questions in racewalking classes are: "How do you racewalk uphill?" and "How do you racewalk down hill?" A hiking gait is the usual method of going uphill in which the springing action of the knees is used for upward propulsion. In going down hill, walkers commonly lean back to counter the pull of gravity.

UPHILL..

1. Your stride shortens going uphill.
2. Do not reach forward with your heel. Let the forward movement of your hips determine your heel placement.
3. Bend your elbows between 90 and 45 degrees depending on the steepness of the hill. A tighter angle raises your center of gravity.
4. To "roll up" a hill, raise your toes higher.
5. Keep your spine straight. Do not bend at the waist as bending promotes bent knees and inhibits hip turn.
6. Keep your buttocks tucked under.

DOWNHILL..

1. Do not lean backwards or semi-sit to offset the pull of gravity.
2. Shorten your stride length slightly to maximize control.
   Do not overstride.
3. Keep your heel close to the ground and let your hips bring your legs forward. Do not raise your knee when bringing your foot forward.
4. Be sure to complete your forward hip turn to lessen heel impact.
5. Open the angle of your elbows up to 120 degrees to lower your center of gravity depending on the steepness of the descent.

COACH BOHDAN BULAKOWSKI

Recovery is extremely important to training. If you do not recover, you cannot train well.

Good training is like walking up steps. You gradually increase the intensity and length of your workouts.

I Poland & America
II What Makes A Coach Good
III Program
IV Training

POLAND AND AMERICA

IN POLAND

Bohdan Bulakowski has been racewalking since 1971. He was a Polish national champion six times. He placed 7th in the 20km at the 1980 Olympics in Moscow and was on the Polish World Cup Team six times in both the 20km and 50km. His best times are: 5km 19:50; 10km 40:40; 20km 1:22:45; 50km 3:53:04. He placed 2nd in the World Masters Championships 20km racewalk in Turku. In Miyasaki, he placed first in both the 5km and 20km (M40) with times of 23:24 and 1:43:34. Entering a new age group (M45), he was first overall in the 20km and 5km as well as first in his Age Division at the Buffalo World Veterans Games.

Bulakowski has been a trainer and coach for 14 years and became the Polish National Team coach in 1989. His team placed 7th in the World Cup in Barcelona, and his top woman walker placed 17th at the Barcelona Olympic Games. As coach, he was responsible for the Polish team's complete program — scheduling, training and technique.

IN AMERICA

Paul Johnson (M55) is one of the masters racewalkers responsible for Bulakowski's American presence. Paul has been coached by Bulakowski since 1993. The following is taken from his interview on April 15, 1995 in La

Grange, Georgia. (For information on Bulakowski's camps, see Appendix.)

From the very first moment I met Bulakowski, I could tell that he was special and that he had something very unique to offer the American racewalking community. With a background devoted to racewalking, he has a full time, 100 percent focus on the sport. Racewalking is all he does. It is all that he wants to do and he has been very successful at it.

After meeting him at Dave McGovern's camp in '93, I tried to think of ways to help him. He had no job. He had no money and he wanted to stay in America. When I got home, I contacted a walking friend of mine, Bill Barnes. Barnes owns the Mountain Harbor resort in Hot Springs, Arkansas, and we decided to put on a racewalking camp to get Bulakowski some money. About 12 people came, and the camp was a great success.

Barnes was so impressed by Bulakowski that he told me emphatically, "We have to help this guy. We have to keep him in this country." Our minds churned for days. As time was running out on Bulakowski's visa, Barnes stepped up and offered to sponsor him for his green card with all the paper work involved.

In sponsoring a nonresident alien Barnes had to put his personal and company assets at risk. He had to sign on the dotted line that he would provide for Bulakowski and keep him off of welfare. Barnes made a two-year commitment to a guy whom he had only known for two days.

There are some other masters involved in this story. Mel Lees of San Luis Obispo, California, and Joe and Dolores Rogers of Atlanta, Georgia, have been especially helpful. All along masters have assisted this man because of who he is, and because of what he could contribute to the senior as well as the masters program.

WHAT MAKES A COACH GOOD?

Bulakowski's special quality as a coach is his genuine interest in your problem. He listens. He never berates you or puts you down. He tries to get his methods across in such a way that you know that your interest is his interest. He is the rare person who does not have an agenda.

When Bulakowski creates a program for an athlete, he carefully considers the personal parameters of the athlete — age, physical condition and problems. A program is not based on hypotheticals such as "This is what you should be doing. This is how fast you should be walking. This is how much weight you should be lifting."

I know some guys who try to get their athletes to do what they think they should do. They are not really tuned in to their athletes' abilities and capabilities. Bulakowski's program is geared to what each athlete, in fact, can do.

Bulakowski genuinely wants to help anyone become a better athlete. He took Allen James, put him on a 50km program and James broke the American record the first time he raced 50km. His methods work. I know from my personal experience as a masters competitor that his methods work.

TOTAL PROGRAM

Bulakowski has many components to his program. If you do his program, you will be successful. If you pick and chose, you will not be as successful.

His warm-up is part of every training session. There are no short cuts. He will not let you take a shortcut. You do the 1km of jogging or walking. You do the mobility drills. You do the technique drills. No ifs or buts. After you do the drills, you do your workout and then you do a cool-down. You do weight work regularly. You rest regularly. You swim regularly. All these parts make the whole program.

Bulakowski completely believes in the importance of bringing an athlete along slowly. He calls it "walking up the steps." He does not allow his athletes to take two steps at a time. If you get injured or falter, you go back a couple of steps and you start up again.

If you were to ask him for a training program, he would want to know how long you have been racewalking and if you have ever trained formally. He would also want to know how many miles you workout, what distances you have raced and what your best times are. In other words, he would want to know your background as well as your present interest and goals. Then he would give you a schedule based on what you have done to keep continuity and steady progression in your training.

For example, someone coming to him for a program with a great deal of experience and in excellent condition would have a different program than someone coming back from an injury or just taking up racewalking after several years away. Bulakowski will never prescribe any uniform number of minutes for everyone. He tailors training to each person's conditioning and heart rate.

TRAINING

(The following is from an interview with Bohdan Bulakowski.)

HEART RATE

One of my fundamentals of training is to monitor the heart rate every single day. It is best to take your pulse the first thing in the morning when you wake up. When you do this, you know how well your body has recovered from your previous workout or race, and what kind of workout you can do that day.

We also check the heart rate after an athlete finishes training. We keep everything in a log book. As the condition of new walkers improves, their heart rates drop. Just as the muscles of the legs strengthen and work more efficiently, so does the heart.

We also use the heart rate for different levels of training. We have four levels of walking. Walk I, Walk II, Speed Work and Racing. If a workout calls for Walk I, the heart rate might be targeted at a range between 120 to 140 for younger walkers and between 110 to 130 for older masters. If a workout then calls for Walk II, the heart rate is targeted at a faster pace, ranging around 145 to 160 for younger walkers and 135 to 150 for older walkers.

Of course, there are outside factors like temperature, humidity, elevation and such that affect the heart rate, and it is necessary to make appropriate adjustments. If you go to an altitude training camp, the first day your heart rate will be higher than normal. It will gradually drop over the following days. After about 10 to 12 days in the altitude, you can start doing good, solid training as your body will be completely acclimated. For the first 10 days you should concentrate on slow technique workouts.

LEVEL I: BASE BUILDING

Each year, you should look at your competition schedule. If you have a major competition in August, January through March should be spent building a solid foundation for speed. This is a period for long distance workouts. If you do not do long distance training, you are not going to be able to perform at a high level of endurance and speed.

Here is an example of a week of basic training. There is always one day off for rest and recovery. If someone has a problem with bent knees, we do not recommend running. We do not recommend running if you have any kind of technique problems. All workouts start with an easy 1-km walk followed by stretching, strengthening exercises and technique drills. It is very important that walkers do sit-ups every day as you need to have strong abdominal and back muscles.

Monday - rest
Tuesday - Walk I - easy, long distance
Wednesday - Easy running moderate heart rate*
Thursday - Walk I - easy long distance
Friday - Short workout of Rhythm & Speed
Saturday - Walk I - each long distance
Sunday - Easy running moderate heart rate*

*You can substitute another type of activity like cross country skiing, swimming, or light weight training for running. Most sports are okay substitutes during this period. I would not recommend any heavy weight lifting, jumping or any sport with a high injury risk. A general rule is to avoid anything that puts extra stress on the muscles. If you have the opportunity to go to a swimming pool after training, this is a good way to relax the muscles. Do not do laps. Just do ten minutes of easy, relaxed swimming.

During this period of basic training, it is important to stay within the heart rate range for Walk I. If you go faster, you lose the physiological benefits of training at the speed of Walk I. For example, if you are 50, your heart rate range is probably between 120-140 for Walk I. If you walk at a 150 heart pace, you are in fact doing Walk II which is closer to the speed of competition and your body is reacting more like it does during competition. Walk I is the basic walk for building a solid foundation. Walk II is a middle process between basic training and racing.

During the period of basic training, you gradually increase the length of the workouts so the basic training in January is shorter than in March. Week after week you increase time and mileage toward a higher level of effort. However, you have to be patient. It is important to take your time and not to try to leap ahead of your body's readiness.

There should be no racing during this period. No competition. This period is for building the foundation. There is some speed work once a week to keep the fast muscles in tone, but that is all.

LEVEL II: BEGINNING COMPETITION

When April comes, it is time to think about competition and to go into the next level of training. You have built the foundation in the first three months of Level I training and are ready to go forward.

During the foundation building we do two easy running days for those who have no technique problems. In the second phase of training, Walk II replaces running. Walk II is very important because you walk much closer to the speed and distance that you do in competition. This walk is like a middle process between basic training and racing. Your body reacts more like it does when racing. Essentially, the purpose of Walk II is to build up distance and build up pace. A typical beginning Level II week would be:

Monday	Rest day
Tuesday	Walk I one hour: heart rate range of 120-140 for younger masters, and 110-130 for older masters.
Wed.	Walk II 1/2 hour: heart rate range of 140-160 for younger masters, 130-150 for older masters.
Thursday	Walk I one hour: as above
Friday	Technique Training with short tempo work
Saturday	Walk I one hour: as above
Sunday	Walk II 1/2 hour: as above
	Remember it is important to stay in the prescribed heart rate ranges for Levels I & II.

Recovery is extremely important to training; if you do not recover, you cannot train well. For example, if you awaken with an elevated pulse rate the day a speed workout is scheduled, do not do the speed work. Cut your workout back immediately and either do light training or rest. The body will let you know.

If you are sick for three or four days, the following three days you should do very light training such as Walk I. Observe yourself. See how you feel. If you are not ready to train, give up and go home. Drink lots of fluid. If you feel fine, you are ready.

A speed workout is a little faster than Walk II. The heart rate should be higher, almost race pace; i.e., 90 to 95 percent. If you are training for a 20km, you do 4 x 3km. In Europe, a 20km for men is a short distance. Or you might do 2km or 1km intervals. If you are doing 2km intervals, you go slower than if you are doing 1km intervals.

DAY BEFORE AND RACE DAY

The day before a race, we always do a warm-up workout. We do exactly the same routine we do before a race, but longer. For example, we might start with an easy 5 minute run, stretch for 10 minutes, do 20 minutes of Walk I with three bursts of 100 meters of speed. If we are not on a track, we might do 1 minute of speed, 1 minute slow, 1 minute of speed and 1 minute slow. After that we cool down with a 5 minute walk and some more stretching.

On race day we warm up and then relax the 10 minutes before race start. You do not want to go to the start line tired. In other words, you do not want to warm up right to the start of a race. If everyone else is rested and you are tired and breathing hard, when the gun goes off, they are gone and you are wondering where they went.

You probably have noticed that some competitors go full out the first 100 meters of a race. In that 30 seconds, they can get their heart rate up to 160. That type of speed burst can tire an athlete for the rest of the race.

During a race it is important to keep in control. Do not go out at a 1:40 lap pace if you cannot hold a 1:40 lap pace. If you can hold a 2:05 pace, do the first lap in 2:05. Go your own pace regardless of what others are doing. The competitor who goes out too fast is going to slow down. If you average your steady pace, you may be surprised to find that there is little difference in your final time and the final time of the person who went out too fast, except that you are not tired and have extra push to win at the end.

In a race, use your head, use your arms and use your legs. When you move your arms well, your legs are going to go well. When you use your head well, you can observe and assess what is happening in the race and can monitor your own pace and strategy. You cannot change your level of training. If someone is a lot better than you, you cannot do anything about that. But you can use your head at any time during a race to assess your resources and the possibilities of passing someone or keeping someone from passing you.

COACH GWEN ROBERTSON

Many times the best conditioned athlete is not the one who wins.

I believe first in working on your strength and then on trying to improve your strength by working on your weakness.

I Overall Approach
II Multi-Paced Training: Tempo, VO2 Max, Speed
III Training Schedule: Race Goals, Peaking
IV The Coach & The Athlete

Gwen Robertson coaches youth and masters athletes in Seattle, Washington. A former member of the Women's National Racewalking Team, Gwen is held in the highest esteem in the racewalking community and has been the team manager of numerous U.S.A. international teams. She coaches Ruth Eberle, her mother, and Bev LaVeck. Both athletes are well-known gold medal winners on the masters competitive circuit.

OVERALL APPROACH

I always try to learn what an athlete's goal is. If a walker's goal is to race and to race well, then that becomes the focus of the training, not just training to train, but training to race.

I have found that many older walkers have never focused on a particular time frame in which they want to race such as the spring or summer months. They just participate in races all year around without any specific goals for peaking.

As a coach, I am a firm believer that it is the athlete's choice how to race, not mine. A goal is what is important. If an athlete wants to race year round, fine. I can set up a plan to do that. However, though such athletes can be good, they may not reach the peak performance they would reach if they focused on one or two big races a year.

I encourage masters to pick a race season and to train for it. I prefer to work with someone who wants to peak for one or two races. Often the big races are in the summer and they can then take an active rest during the holiday months.

I definitely feel that a period of rest is psychologically necessary to avoid burn out. Not only does the body need to rest, the mind needs to rest. A mental break from the day in and day out routine of getting out the door and training is rejuvenating. When training starts again, everyone is raring to go.

Active rest does not mean sitting and doing nothing. My athletes are encouraged to stay active with cross-country skiing, biking, swimming, running and to enjoy the activities that they have not been able to do because of their training schedule.

I consider one month an optimal rest period, particularly the month of December. This is a month when a lot of things are going on. Training starts again in January. An athlete might take a one to two week vacation in the middle of the summer, too. It is sometimes hard to train when you are away from home. One or two weeks of active rest in the middle of a racing season does not hurt. Often athletes will come back better than they were before.

MULTI-PACED TRAINING

In the last several years, I have changed to what the British call a multi-paced training year in which athletes do all kinds of speeds. For example, they will do some fast training early in the season to keep in touch with their fast twitch muscle fibers. This means doing the same type of fast work in January they do in June, but only once a week or once every two weeks rather than twice a week.

I have noticed that athletes seem to recover better from training and from racing using this multi-paced method. Combining shorter fast workouts, longer fast workouts, tempo workouts and $V0_2$ max workouts provides a good mental break as they are not doing the same thing over and over.

**TEMPO WORKOUT

A tempo workout is 10 to 15 seconds per mile slower than a walker's current 10km race pace. It is for increasing your anaerobic threshold.

You want to do this for 30 minutes or so. Tempo work is one of the most critical workouts you can do and it should be included year round.

With older athletes, I basically have gone to two hard days a week, occasionally three in the racing season. One of these quality sessions could well be a tempo workout, a 6 to 7 mile workout with 2 to 3 miles in the middle at tempo pace.

You would not want to start right out with this. You might start by doing a 15 minute warm-up walk, a 15 minute tempo walk and a 15 minute cool-down. If this goes well, you can gradually increase to 2 miles of moderate walking, 3 miles of tempo and another mile of easy walking. If you are training for a longer distance like a 20km, you might get up to a 40-45 minute tempo walk; but again, it is at a pace 10 to 15 seconds per mile slower than your 10km race pace.

As your fitness increases, you want to do a time trial or race every two to three months to check your tempo pace. If your race pace has increased, you want to adjust your tempo speed. If you do a 5km race, you can figure out your 10km pace with this formula: 2 x 5km time plus 1:30 to 2:00. For example: If you do a 5km in 25:00, your 10km time would be 51:30 to 52:00 and your mile pace approximately 8:20. Your tempo pace would be 10 to 15 seconds per mile slower or between 8:30 and 8:35 per mile.

VO_2 MAX & LONG WORKOUTS

Another quality workout would be a $V0_2$ max workout at your 5km race pace. Frequently, you will see this workout written 5 x 5 x 5 (5 times 5 minutes with a 5 minute recovery between efforts.) You do not really kick into the aerobic phase until after the first two minutes. It is a very hard workout. For masters athletes, the 5 minute workout is somewhere near 800 meters to 1000 meters; of course, there is an age factor here. However, as an athlete gets in better condition, I think the speed interval can be increased to 6 or 7 minutes at race pace. Total distance should be 3 miles or about 10 percent of your weekly mileage.

I think it is important to do long distance workouts. There are some athletes who thrive on speed work and there are some athletes who thrive on longer work. I think athletes need some of each. However, I believe in working on your strength first, and then on trying to improve your strength by working on your weakness. Many hold just the opposite philosophy. They work on their weakness more. I recommend that if you thrive on long distance workouts, do one a week. If you do not, do one every other week or even one every three weeks if you are racing.

When you sit down and plan out your week, you may find that there are not enough days to do everything. If you have a race and you are only racewalking five days a week, you may find that you can only schedule one other quality session that week. It is easier to fit in all the helpful elements if you are training six days a week.

SPEED WORK & INTERVALS

For those who really like speed work, they can do a $V0_2$ max in conjunction with a short, fast workout with 1-minute repeats that are near maximum speed. This is especially good for a 5km or 10km race.

The danger of injury with a lot of really fast work is an important consideration, especially if you are older and do not allow proper recovery the two days after the speed workout. Short, fast workouts can be incredibly fatiguing. If you are a long distance type and your muscles are not used to moving fast, you are very vulnerable to injury. A little fast work goes a long way.

We generally do anywhere from 30 seconds to 2 minutes of maximum paced speed work, but I think 2 minutes is long to be going near maximum. Generally 45 to 90 seconds is good with at least the same amount of recovery. So if you do 60 seconds fast; you take 60 to 90 seconds for recovery. Fatigue starts to build up pretty rapidly. Masters should not do more than 8 minutes total at a maximum pace. That is not very many minutes, but the lactic acid builds up in the muscles. I use this workout the least, probably once every three weeks.

Interval workouts consist of repetitions of specific distances with a rest between. For example, you do 8 x 400m laps 5 seconds per lap faster than your 5km race pace. This workout is not as difficult as the short, maximum speed workouts above. It can be used in a week when you are going to race. You recover from this fairly quickly.

SUMMARY OF WORKOUTS

Tempo	Every week, 10-15 seconds per mile slower than 10km pace.
VO_2 Max	Every week to every other week, 5km race pace.
Speed	Every 3 weeks, 10-12 seconds faster than 5km race pace.
Intervals	400m, 5 seconds per lap faster than 5km race pace.
Distance	Every or every other week; 9-12 miles for a 10km race.

TRAINING SCHEDULE

When it comes to the number of days masters should workout in a week, I am conservative. I think masters walkers need plenty of recovery time. Masters can do the quality work, but it takes them longer to recover from hard races or hard workouts than it does a younger person.

It is not unusual to see masters steadily improving when suddenly the bottom falls out. Why? They have been impressed by the idea that the more hard workouts the better. When they reach a certain level of accumulated fatigue, they start spiraling downward.

I am a firm believer in one or two rest days a week. It is not unusual for slightly injured athletes to come back after a layoff of three to four days and make P.R.'s. They are rested and more relaxed. Once you experience this, you do not worry about taking a day off.

The compulsive athlete has a problem moderating. Endurance athletes are often compulsive. They think about the other guy being out there training and feel they have to be out there training more. It is fairly easy to get into this syndrome.

I am not concerned too much about mileage. Mileage is just something that is easy to quantify and that is why we get stuck measuring our progress with miles. "Oh, I did 40 miles last week. This week I did 42 miles so I am doing better." This is not necessarily true if you are not doing the right workout elements. It is just like Ian Whatley said about the national team walkers. "It's not that the Americans are not good enough or that they do not train. It's that they do not necessarily put it together right. We are working hard, but we are not necessarily doing the right combinations of things."

In summary, my overall view of training is: In January, as my walkers come off their rest period, their mileage is lower and their speed is slower. I will have them do a maximum speed workout once a month and by May, twice a month. Same with repetitions. Early in January I may have them do two tempo workouts of 1 1/2 miles working up to 3 miles, or I may have them do a tempo and $V0_2$ max workout.

Once a week or twice a month, they may do a long walk of 8 to 12 miles. All the other days are "recovery days" of 4 to 7 miles at 1:30 to 2:00 slower than the walker's 10km race pace per mile. This is a good aerobic training walk. It allows recovery for the next hard workout.

It is always important to ask yourself, "How do I really feel today?" Sometimes you may feel sluggish before you warm up. Then, after you have warmed up and have gotten into stride, you may say, "I feel all right and am ready to hit it." If you do not feel all right and do a hard workout when you are not ready, the workout is not going to do you any good. You risk getting sick, injured or stale.

You have to be flexible with your training. Let's say you have the elements that you want to fit into a two week cycle and you end up doing them in a 17-day cycle, so what? It is better for you to be flexible. Some people may be able to do the same workouts in a 12-day cycle. Everybody recovers differently, and recovery from certain workouts is harder for some people than for others.

Many people use their pulse rate before they get out of bed in the morning to assess if they have recovered from the previous day's workout. I do not have my athletes do that. Knowing how you feel physically is a sufficient clue. When you are tired, you know it. When you are physically ready to go, you know it. Sometimes you may not be mentally ready, but you are physically ready.

PACING AND RACING

I am a firm believer in feel. Your training should teach you how your body feels at different speeds. A watch gives you the feedback to correlate pace and time. The objective is to get to know the level of physical intensity you feel at your race pace. If you really know what your race pace feels like, you can do it any day of the week. Holding pace is critical in any endurance event. My athletes have time goals so that they know what their pace should be per lap or per mile. Many athletes want to go out hard the first mile to get a 15 or 20 second cushion on their competition. Then they blow up. They cannot hold on to the pace. If a walker puts 15 seconds in the bank at the beginning, but is 30 seconds slower at the end, what has she or he gained by sprinting off the start line? Why not go 10 seconds slower at the beginning and 30 seconds faster at the end?

You learn to control a race by training. You do tempo work. You do $V0_2$ max work and you learn to pace. You do intervals or repetitions, and you learn to pace. If you do all these workouts, you should develop an inner clock that tells you how fast you are going.

I do not want my athletes using heart monitors during a race. I think racing is a physical contest on a particular day. In other words, athletes should be able to sense how fast they are going and whether they can keep up their pace for 5km or 10km. Maybe they will not keep up their pace, but this inability does not mean a heart monitor would have changed the outcome. I think competition should be head-to-head competition on a specific day at given altitude, temperature and humidity. Competition is what two athletes can do in a moment of time.

The Kick: My athletes sometimes ask me about sprinting the last 100 or 200 meters. This is often called "the kick." "Kicking" at the end of a race is mainly mental. There is some physical element to it, of course, but I do not spend time on kicking. The kick will be there for athletes if they have done their speed work and trained well.

If you go out too fast, or if you try going at a faster pace than your training supports, no matter how much you want the kick to be there, it will not be. However, if you walk a good, steady, consistent pace, even if it is a P.R. pace, you will be able to find a little something extra provided you have done the elements of training that lay the foundation for it. That is why I have become a real believer in multi-paced training.

PEAKING

A lot is being written about peaking. Peaking is both mental and physical. They are equal components. In order to peak, everything in your life needs to be going pretty well. If there is an emotional or mental drag on you, I do not care how badly you want a peak performance, it is going to be very difficult to do one. Throughout your preparatory five month cycle, you want to be getting your life in order so you can relax during the time period when you want to have peak races. You do not want to be fighting with your husband or wife or anyone. You do not want problems at work. Keep the psychological and physical stresses low.

Peaking involves a significant cutback in mileage, as much as 50 percent. I have seen some coaches recommend 60 percent. If you usually do 30 miles in a week, you would do 15 miles. At the same time, it is important to keep in touch with your fast twitch muscles. You need to do some race-pace type intervals during the last several weeks. If you are racing during this peak period, you are getting in a good hard effort, but that is not enough. Doing 400 meter intervals at a 5km pace is good as they are not stressful or tiring. You can recover quickly and feel good.

As your mileage cuts down, you eliminate all junk. You warm up, workout, cool down, but you do not worry about mileage. What happens after a few days? You tell your coach, "Boy I have a lot of energy." You feel great and happy and start champing at the bit for race day to come. When it does, you are ready. You just relax and let it happen.

How long you taper depends on what time of year it is and how broad your base is. If a target race is early in the year, maybe the taper will only be a day or two, but that is not really a taper. That is simply getting ready for the race. The taper before a key race is probably two weeks. The first week may have a 30 percent reduction in mileage while the second week may have a 50 to 60 percent reduction. The purpose of a two-week taper is to reduce all physical and mental pressure from your workouts so you can relax and be maximally prepared for your big race.

THE COACH & THE ATHLETE

I think everyone should have a coach to help them compartmentalize some of the stresses and keep them focused on their goals. I want my athletes to be mentally relaxed so they can really benefit from their workouts. The same is true before a race. Athletes who are performing at their top levels are very relaxed. They will not race well if they are thinking about what they should be doing rather than focusing on what they are doing.

It is harder for competitive athletes with job and family stresses. Some days, it is not possible to take care of all the pressing demands. At such times,

I tell my athletes not to worry about their workouts. I feel it is better for them to take the hour or hour and a half they would ordinarily give to a workout and do what they need to do. If skipping a workout now and then allows an athlete to sleep better and to avoid feeling he or she has to get 15 hours of activity into 12 hours, fine.

In other words, I give my athletes permission to take time off as there are times when life just gets in the way of training. My mother (Ruth Eberle) is a prime example. She does not train like a lot of people do, but she does the right things when she does. Maybe her mileage is not where it could be, but it does not matter. She is a teacher, a wife, mother and grandmother, and she has many important things to do in a day. If all her commitments are in balance, the amount of training she does will be done well and she will race well.

I very seldom worry about athletes taking too much time off. I think that adults are racewalking because they really want to racewalk. Sometimes kids take the easy way because they are not sure what they want. But by and large, a mature athlete will not. The bottom line is desire.

There is another side to flexibility with workouts. If an athlete has had a stressful week and has taken two or three days off, it is important for the coach to say, "That's okay. However, this week we are not going to do anything new. We are going to stick to last week's plan." This way athletes will not overdo and get into a situation where they get tired because they are trying to make up for lost training. An athlete should not do 20 extra miles because of missing 20 miles the week before.

Many times the best conditioned athlete is not the one who wins. There is no way of proving this, but have you ever wondered how an athlete won a race on the amount of training he or she was doing? The answer may be that such athletes are relaxed and have done enough of what is needed to race well.

A coach is a mirror. I believe that I am there for my athletes to see themselves, and that it is my job to be honest with them. My athletes must be confident that if I tell them they are looking great, they are looking great; or if I tell them they need some rest, they will accept my judgment and not take it negatively. Frequently it is hard for athletes to back off, yet backing off at times may be the very thing that brings success to their racing.

The long-term process of training is very important to success, especially for endurance events. The number of years that you have put into good training will pay off. When I take on new people, I tell them to give the sport six months to one year and to let me make the judgment calls. Athletes have to be confident in their coach and feel that their coach knows what he or she is doing. In turn, coaches have to get to know their athletes because each athlete is different and they have to understand each one. It can take up to one year. From there it is a four year plan.

If an athlete does not have a plan for development, it is hit and miss. If you know where you are going and where you want to be, you have a better chance of getting there. You get out what you put in. There are no secrets. There is no magic. It is planning and hard consistent work. It is getting your whole life to fit into your plan. Helping athletes keep focused on their plans is what makes the job of the coach important.

COACH MIKE DEWITT

My coaching philosophy is "train, but do not strain."

I am not the most technical coach around. A lot of my coaching is, "Let's see what I can do with you."

I Coaching Philosophy
II The Competitive Spirit - Motivation
III Technique
IV Training Schedules - Summer, Fall, Winter
V Shoes

Mike DeWitt is the running and racewalking coach at the University of Wisconsin Parkside. He is also an active competitor. In 1984, he placed 8th in the 50km Olympic Trials; in 1988, he placed 10th; and in 1992, 9th. His best 50km time is 4:22:23. His best 20km time is 1:30:40. For the last decade, Coach DeWitt has been America's primary coach of young elite racewalkers. He has had over 30 N.A.I.A. All American walkers, 20 athletes in the Olympic Trials, and four Olympians—Jim Heiring, Andrew Kaestner, Debbi Lawrence and Michelle Rohl. He also has an enthusiastic masters team who combine serious training and fun.

COACHING PHILOSOPHY

My coaching philosophy is built on my own experience. I have been a competitor for over 25 years. I competed in high school, have never stopped competing, and would like to be able to continue as long as I can. I have never been really hurt and have trained every week. I have done the long, slow distance walks, putting in 100-mile weeks. I have done only speedwork and not much else. Name the combination, I have done it.

I was a senior in college when they introduced a 3000 meter walk into competition. I walked the 3km in 13:57 to make All American at that distance. Now, I can walk a 3km around 13:00 minutes. This improvement reflects the improved technique training I have had since my early racewalking years. When I have finished coaching athletes in college, I expect them to continue getting better and faster for a number of years.

My coaching philosophy is "train, but do not strain." I take into account that athletes have lives. It is good to be motivated and to have one focus in your life, but that is not the way I am. My focus is split between being an elementary school teacher all day, a college coach from 4 to 6 p.m., and a dad and husband in the evening. I strongly believe that it is necessary to take care of the important things in your life to get the most out of yourself athletically. My whole life is founded on my athletic background of doing the best job I can and of being in good enough shape to do all the things there are to do in a day.

THE COMPETITIVE DRIVE

Competitiveness is individual. Personally, I do not consider myself an overly aggressive athlete. I basically make sure that I go as fast as I can. When it comes down to racing, particularly in longer races, if someone is in front of me, I am going to go after him. But if that person outdoes me, I do not worry about it.

I try to instill a desire in my athletes to do their best. I tell them, "Don't beat yourself. If you do your best, you will be pretty successful over the long range."

I am pretty good at knowing how fast my athletes can walk, so I set them up that way. They know if I tell them that they can walk at a certain speed, they should be able to walk pretty close to that speed, if not faster.

I remember one of my coaches telling me, "You should walk this fast." It was faster than I thought I could go, significantly faster than I thought I could go. It shook my confidence in him.

With my athletes, I say, "Hey. You are doing these workouts. You should be able to go that fast racing, too." They can see that. I give them a logical, pragmatic look at their ability. I tell each one realistically, "You should be able to make this time, so make sure you do it. If you do it, you will be able to go home and not worry."

The athletes who are very competitive, who really want to be good, have to learn race strategy. If they are not very talented, I can teach them how to race at an even pace and finish a little stronger. If they are naturally talented, I teach them how to control a race and win.

One of the most important aspects of race strategy is knowing your competition well. This knowledge allows you to set a race plan and to put yourself in a position to win the race.

Winning may be a matter of speed or it may be a matter of finish place. First place is nice, but look at the awards closely. In the N.A.I.A. Championships, the second through sixth place plaques all say "All-American" on them. In the USATF outdoor nationals, second through tenth place all bring national team membership. The message I give is: If you are not exactly where you want to be in a race, make sure you are in the top six or top ten.

MOTIVATION

When I train very talented walkers, my coaching is more specific. The bigger the race, the better they do. They are very self-motivated and have a lot of self-confidence. They also are very coachable. When they are told that they should be able to finish a race in a certain place or to make a certain time, they will feel they can and will do it. The four Olympians I have coached have all been like that. The important point here is that their training made these expectations reasonable, and they knew it.

MIKE AND MICHELLE ROHL ON THE DEWITT COACHING STYLE *(August 18, 1992, just after Michelle's 20th place finish in the 10km Walk at the Barcelona Olympics.)*

Michelle Rohl: Coach DeWitt told me I could finish in the top 20 in Barcelona and I did! I had a long-term plan and knew my workout schedule right up to the race. My coach knows more about what I am doing than I do. I look at my schedule, see what my pace is to be, and how long I am to do it. At every race, he gives me a place goal and a race plan which I follow.

In Barcelona, I was supposed to go out in the middle of the pack. He told me the pack would probably go out fast, and it did go out relatively quickly, but not as quickly as I expected. He said to keep an even pace and if I felt like going fast the first half, to hold back. He also told me that if I did not feel like going fast in the second half, to go fast anyway. He said I would have to make negative splits to pass people because no one slows down at the Olympics. He also told me to concentrate on good form.

Mike Rohl: The famous hill back to the stadium in Barcelona had a 5.8 percent grade. It was about 1400 meters long. The trick was to hold pace as much as possible. The women leaders must have known that they had to save something for the hill. Based on their split times of around 21:00 at the World Cup and World Championships, they were about 1:15 slower. They came through the 5km in Barcelona in 22:15 and about 20 walkers went by in the next 15 seconds. Michelle went by at 22:46 and was 30th. That is how close the women were. The temperature was 93 degrees and the humidity was 41 percent. The first woman crossed the finish line in 44:30. Michelle finished in 46:45.

Coach DeWitt's strength is seen in the consistency of his training. He wants his walkers to be able to perform consistently on any type of course in any kind of climate. For Michelle to have kept to a time of 46:45 with a hill like the walkers faced in Barcelona is a tribute to her training.

TECHNIQUE TRAINING

I am not the most technical coach around. I coach by feel and coach each person a little differently. There are a few general principles, but they cannot be applied in the same way to everyone. There are many different body types.

For example, when walking really started changing and the Mexican style started coming in with all the drills and exercises, I realized that there was no way that I could walk like the Mexicans. I can try all I want, but I am too tight. If I work on it, I may be able to improve my flexibility some. However, every time I do a lot of stretching, drills and exercises, I start having hamstring or calf problems. As I am not flexibly built, I must walk as efficiently as I can with what I have.

Some walkers need to work on the forward lean to be legal and have to spend extra time on it. However, if your body is not built to lean a certain way, then I am not going to make you lean that way unless there is something you can strengthen that will help. Michelle has such a swayback she cannot lean forward. She cannot strengthen her abdominals as she cannot do sit-ups. She can do crunches some, but that is about it.

If I can get my athletes to a point where they are close to walking the way they are supposed to walk, that is fine. If an athlete's style looks right for them, I go with it.

Turnover: The important part of technique is turnover. Turnover is important for all ages and we do fartleks on hills to improve turnover. I tell my athletes, "The better turnover you have, the less stride length matters. If you can get a fast turnover and a long stride length, you are going to be great."

Knees: One of the hardest technique challenges involves knee straightening. Some walkers cannot get their knees straight because of injury, age or surgery. I tell them, "We will try to make your knees as good as we can." A lot of my coaching is, "Let's see what I can do with you."

Ankle flexibility is the biggest factor in having a straight knee. You have to land with your toes up as much as possible when your heel contacts the ground. Standing at attention with your heels on the ground and toes up is a good starter. Doing some ankle work with weights helps. Toe raises, squats and other exercises that increase the range of motion of the ankle help.

Reaching from the hips also helps in getting your heel down and toes up. This move requires you to improve hip flexibility. If you do hip flexibility drills regularly, you will notice a difference. Weights may be used to strengthen weak areas. At the same time, it is important to watch out for increasing stress on the hamstrings. They are the most frequently injured walking muscles.

MASTERS TRAINING SCHEDULES

This masters training schedule assumes that the longest competitive racing distance will be 10km. It is for athletes who can score 60% or higher on the "Age Graded Tables."

Monday: Easy fitness type walking. Alternatives: exercise bike, run, swim, or simply an off day.

Tuesday: 30 to 45 minutes of easy racewalking at a pace about 1 minute per mile slower than recent best 5km pace.

Wed: Tough training day: Between 2 to 3 miles of intensity work." For example:

(a) 10 x 400m at a 1500m or faster pace with a 90 second to a 2-minute rest.

(b) 4-5 x 800m at a 3km pace with a 3-5 minute rest.

(c) 3km-5km starting 30 seconds slower than best pace for the first kilometer down to race pace by the last.

Thursday: 45 minutes "how you feel fartleks" meaning if you feel strong, get in a good solid fartlek workout, or if you are tired from Wednesday's efforts, just go through your gears comfortably. For every pickup, you rest by walking easy the same amount of time.

Friday: Exactly the same as Monday. It is an easy day or off day, walker's choice.

Saturday: Trial or race day: If a race day, a full effort is planned and set up. If a trial day, then it is:

(a) A regular 3km or 5km at 15 seconds or so per mile slower than recent best effort.

(b) A 2km at a 3km pace.

(c) A 4km at a 5km pace.

Sunday: (a) A 10km for 60-90 minutes at a pace 1-2 minutes per mile slower than recent best 3km time.

(b) For marathon - Build up schedule from 2 to 4 1/2 hours starting out 9 weeks before the marathon.

There is no given pace but an 11:00 per mile pace is the fastest recommended.

For Elite Masters, a longer tempo workout is a good training workout. A tempo workout for 10km, 20km and 50km is between 6 to 15 miles. For example:

A 10km tempo walk would be 1-6-1: 1-mile easy warm-up, a 6-mile workout, followed by a 1-mile cool-down. The six miles may be 20 to 30 seconds per mile off your 10km or 20km time. You may have a range of 15 seconds more or less, but you should not walk faster or slower than that pace. A group of walkers doing a 1-6-1 on a given day would all be walking different speeds. A mile can be added to the workout every one or two weeks. For example, 1-7-1, 1-8-1. A 10km walker may only go up to a 1-7-1 tempo workout. A 20km walker may only go up to a 1-10-1. A 50km walker may go up to 15 or 18 miles.

The purpose of this tempo workout is to build endurance over a long period of time at a definite pace.

For most masters, a 1-4-1 tempo workout is enough since the longest distance most masters chose to race is 10km. The goal of a longer tempo workout becomes "survive!"

WINTER TRAINING

In Wisconsin, winter is a time to either concentrate 100% on the speed races of the indoor track season, or on getting to a warm climate marathon. Because of some of the great indoor training facilities in Southeast Wisconsin, both plans can be accomplished very successfully.

For those hammering out indoor speed racing, the key is "perfect" technique. Walking hard and fast once a week and being critically judged by a video camera or by a coach are musts. You need to know your technique breaking point. Many times master walkers are in shape to go faster than their technique will allow them.

In order to walk well indoors, you really need to get to an indoor track at least once a week for training. Then you need to race regularly, two or three times a month during January, February, and March. Indoor track is really about the most fun season because the meets are generally shorter than outdoors, the closeness and noise level is usually a good motivator, and the "weather" is always good inside!

Getting ready for a nice weather marathon can be a real challenge, too. The biggest key to walking outdoors in cold winter weather is knowing how to dress. It really is not a matter of arctic gear. All you need is some good polypropylene underwear and a good light wind resistant warm up suit. (Gore-tex is the best.) Wear layers of clothes that are absorbent because you can sweat just as much in the winter as you do in the summer. A good hat with a chin protector is a must. If you wear glasses, you need to keep the covering around your eyes a little loose to avoid frosting up. Wearing two pairs of mittens and good polypro socks also help to keep you warm.

The place you walk is also important. Walking in the city is much better than in the country because you have many more natural and man-made wind blocks to help shield you. Be sure to check the wind direction. You should go out into the wind as much as possible so that you can come back with the wind behind you. If you go out on a wet and cold day, make sure you keep your loops short in distance in case you get real cold and wet. This way you are only ten minutes away from a hot shower!

Of course, you can always go into a big mall early in the morning or into an indoor facility and walk in circles for hours at a time. This is better for those who really hate cold weather.

Winter is a good time to get in a lot of good quality miles. Remember you are not at the North Pole. Even though the weather can get rotten at times, it often is in the 20 to 40 degree range and the roads are clear.

SUMMER TRAINING

Summer weather in the Midwest is always a consideration. Knowing how to deal with heat and changing conditions is critical to your success and enjoyment in training and racing. Here are a few tips on how to keep motivated as it gets warmer.

Hydrate! Drink plenty of water and fluids, especially on days when you know that you have a hard workout planned. That means hydrating the day before as well as the day of the workout or race. During the workout or race, drink a steady flow of water and replacement drinks. Research has shown how essential fluid replacement is to performance levels. It is just as important to keep drinking after an event. Drink until you feel saturated and your urine is "clear" as opposed to darker yellow.

Dress appropriately! Clothing that is light in color and weight is the rule here. Consider how hot it is and what your tolerance to heat and humidity is. You should wear 100% cotton T-shirts as much as possible for they hold your perspiration longer and that keeps you cooler. Wearing tank tops is also good, but remember that the sun's energy on your skin can heat you up pretty fast, faster than a heavy T-shirt will in most cases.

Carefully pick your training time and routes! During hot weather, it is very important to pick the time of day that you train. I have always preferred evening workouts during the summer months. As your body is getting hotter, the air is generally cooling down. In the morning as you start getting hot, so does the air. You can do a lot to protect yourself in the summer by choosing courses that are shaded and near water stops.

Adjust your pace to the heat! Adjusting your pace is an important part of race strategy in hot weather. Use a rough guideline of adding one second per mile onto your best race pace for every degree above 70 degrees if the humidity is under 66 percent. Add one second per mile for every 5 percent humidity above 66 percent If you get above 15 seconds of adjustments, forget about racing or doing a hard workout.

FALL TRAINING

The fall is the best time of the year for training and racing the longer distances. You are in great shape from a summer of track meets and quick work. Your turnover rate is at its best for the year. The weather is cooler and you can increase your Sunday walks without fear of getting sun burn, drying up, blowing away or melting in a humid oven.

Workouts should be designed to be "comfortable" in the fall. Races should physically challenge your ability to hold on and finish a race that takes one, two and sometimes even three or four hours to complete. I like to think of long races as masters' lessons in appreciation for what Olympians do when they compete in the 20km and 50km racewalks.

So, for those of you who are a little shy about walking beyond 10Km, make the fall a time for challenging yourself. Do the longer distances and reach for a personal achievement or a gold medal. Long distance racing will make you an elite performer. It will put you in the top 500 or better in the world.

SHOES

Personally, I like very low heeled shoes. If I were to make a racewalking shoe, I would have the bottom cut out. I would have my heel right on the ground. The lower the shoes, the better for me. I think low heels help a lot of walkers, especially the ones who have a problem getting their toes up. I tell them to find the lowest shoes around and to take the insoles out, anything to get them down on the ground so they can get their toes up a little more.

I am not talking about a negative heel necessarily, but flat for sure and a nice solid heel counter. I think these are the features that make a good shoe. Elevated heels hurt walkers who have a hard time getting their toes up. We used to have heels on our shoes. If we put them on our shoes again, it might help keep the elite walkers on the ground for a short time, but I do not think heels will really slow them down or make them more legal.

COACH MARTIN RUDOW

An important concept in racewalking is that your arm swing is directly related to the length of your stride.

Height and leg length are of zero importance to racewalking.

I Three Technique Tips - Arm Swing, Stride, Swayback
II Straight Knee Rule

Martin Rudow is a nationally respected coach and IAAF judge. He has written the IAAF official racewalking text, *Advanced Racewalking*. His new video, *Maximum Walking*, is for fitness walkers and combines his personal narration on technique training with exemplary footage of racewalkers. For information on his book and video tape, see Appendix.

TECHNIQUE TIPS

ARM SWING:

An important concept in racewalking is that the arm swing is directly related to the length of the stride. I might say to an athlete we have to work on lengthening or shortening your stride. The way to do this is to focus on your arm swing as your legs will follow your arm swing exactly. As long as your right hand is swinging forward, your left foot is going to come forward. The moment your right hand stops swinging forward, your left heel is going to make contact with the ground. When your right hand stops moving back, your rear or left foot is going to come off the ground.

Everyone can find their ideal stride length by working their arms through a definite range of motion. To do this, your shoulders must be relaxed. You want your arms to work at your waistband from your hand to your elbow, keeping the elbow close to the body. You simply cannot do this if your shoulders are tense. The faster you swing your arms, the faster your legs will go.

The arm swing should never rise above the lower breastbone nor cross the midline of the body. If you watch walkers side view and see their hands going behind them, their swing is too far back. The hands should go no farther back than the line of the buttocks, and go no farther forward than around five inches. This is the range of motion which will control your stride length and let you maximize legality and power.

The other part of the arm motion is at the waistband. The movement is low, forward and back, as opposed to sideways. Let your elbows go side-to-side and see what it does to your hips. Your hips will go side-to-side, too. Drive the elbows straight back and your hips go back and forth without wasting energy. Proper arm action helps propel you forward.

STRIDE:

Everyone wants to have the right stride length for his or her body build and height. Many people say, "Gee, Mr. Rudow, you must be a natural for racewalking. You have long legs and a long stride." Height and leg length are of zero importance to racewalking. What is important is turnover, strides per minute, and keeping your stride at its ideal length for you. Turnover, not longer steps, is how to generate legal speed.

Ivanenko from Russia, the gold medalist in the 50km in Seoul, is 5 feet 4 inches. Batista of Mexico, probably the greatest 20km walker ever, is around 5 feet 5 inches. Another top walker from Spain, Jose Marin, is 5 feet 2 inches. There are also walkers who are 5 feet 10 inches and 6 feet. Maybe in an ideal world, if you were 6 feet 10 inches with the stride frequency of Batista, you would be the ideal walker!

SWAYBACK: *(The following is adapted from the section on Swayback in Martin's book,* Advanced Racewalking.*)* A swayback is the visible inward curve of the lower spine. It is a postural problem caused by weak lower abdominal muscles and tight lower back muscles. It creates many technique problems as it inhibits the vertical and horizontal hip action.

The common way of correcting swayback is to strengthen the lower abdominal muscles and increase lower back flexibility. However, sit-ups, the most frequently prescribed exercise, may do more harm than good. Most forms of sit-ups strengthen the hip flexor muscles and tighten lower back muscles. This result causes even greater forward pressure on the lower spine.

To correct swayback, do specific lower back stretches and lower abdominal muscles strengtheners. Pelvic tilts and curl-ups with and without rotation are specific for this purpose. Doing these exercises should be the primary goal of any serious racewalker with a swayback.

THE "NEW" STRAIGHT LEG RULE

New Rule: The advancing leg must be straightened (i.e. not bent at the knee) from the moment of first contact with the ground until in the vertical upright position.

With the recent extension of the straight knee rule to include the distance from heel contact to the upright position, I urge all masters walkers to do two things: (1) Warm up well. (2) Do not make any wild surges at the end of a race.

I turned in three red cards in the last 100 yards of a race recently. In each case, the offending walkers were bending their knees to increase speed to pass someone. Judges just cannot let this infraction go, but it bothers me when walkers have otherwise been walking fairly all race long.

I also note that many masters come from a running background. As a result their hip flexors are tight and quads overly developed for walking. This gives them a tendency to take too long a stride to the front. When they do this, they often flatten their lead foot well in front of their body, and this contributes to soft knees. Solution: Build hip flexor flexibility, work on hips and shoulder rotation, and cut the front stride.

I wish that walkers fully understood how much we judges hate to throw people out of races. With the new rule, we cannot allow compromise with soft knees. Help us by developing better technique! You will go faster and we will not have to DQ anyone. My ideal race would be to turn in no red cards.

WORKOUTS

STRETCHING / STRENGTHENING FOR GOOD TECHNIQUE

IAN WHATLEY
RON LAIRD
DAVE MCGOVERN
RICHARD CHARLES
SHIRLEY CAPPS
JACK BRAY

COMMON INJURIES

BERNIE FINCH, D.C.

Ian Whatley (top), Dave McGovern (middle), Richard Charles (bottom)

IAN WHATLEY

Since "talent" is largely defined by genetics, training is the route to better racing performances.

I Training
- **Supramaximal Workout**
- **VO_2 Max Workout**
- **Lactate Acid Threshold Workout - Tempo, Bursts**
- **Long Distance Walking & Easy Walking**

II Training
- **Plyometrics**
- **Heart Rate Monitors**
- **Tire Dragging**

Ian Whatley has been the Sports Science Representative of the National Racewalking Committee since 1992 and the author of numerous Racewalking Sports Science Bulletins. He graduated from Loughborough University in England with a degree in Bioengineering and was brought to the US by NIKE on a unique skills visa to set up an applied research section in the 1980s. He holds 23 patents. A member of the Men's National Team, he has represented the US internationally in the 20km outdoor walk and 3km indoor walk. He is a regular coach at Dave McGovern's clinics and camps, and is the author of "Ian & Dave's low budget Racewalking videos." (See Appendix.)

MAKING EVERY STEP COUNT

INTRODUCTION

Fast racing comes from the combination of talent with hard physical training. Since "talent" is largely defined by genetics, training is the route to better racing performances.

There is a volume of training beyond which damage rather than improvement occurs. This volume is termed overtraining and limits the total training load tolerable. This means that every step of every training session needs to be as effective as possible in improving racing ability. The following are some guidelines:

- Know what works for you. Individuals differ and there is no one training regime that will affect all athletes in the same way. Learn as much as you can about training, but balance this with experiments to see how different stresses affect your body.

- Set goals and work towards them. Every training session should have a purpose which leads towards a long-term objective. You must always be able to answer the question "What is the purpose of this training session?"

- Focus on good technique. Every step you take must be efficient and legal or you are learning bad habits and wasting your workouts.

- Learn speed. You cannot run a 4:00 mile if you cannot run a quarter in sub 60 seconds. Masters cannot walk a 20km in 1:40:00 or a 10km in 50:00 unless they can walk a kilometer in 5 minutes.

- Focus on your "perceived exertion." Perceived exertion is a scientific term for how hard a work load feels. Your brain integrates all incoming information and says, for example, "I am working about 17 out of 19 at the moment." You are not even conscious of this evaluative process. Your body passes on clues like your heart rate, breathing rate, blood acidity, body temperature and local muscle stretching. Your mind puts the information together to come to an assessment. If you are working out at a high level of discomfort, this assessment may be, "This is very hard work. I am going to stop." A different work load could give medium discomfort and register as "I'm not really enjoying this, but I can go on."

THE FIVE KEY TRAINING VELOCITIES

SUPRA MAXIMAL WORKOUT

Objective: Improved economy of walking technique.
Velocity: Peak velocity for 100 to 200 meters.
Time: Work periods of 20 to 50 seconds with full recovery.

To me a supra maximal workout means standing on a line, mentally focusing and saying, "OK, here's my technique. This is exactly how I am going to do it. Go." You are moving as fast as you can without your form becoming severely illegal. It is an extremely short burst in which you may not even have time to breathe. What you are trying to do is get your muscles twitching as fast as they can, and it will feel as though your legs are trying to keep up.

Between bursts, you take full recovery. Some athletes may need 90 seconds or 2 to 5 minutes. Recovery is when you feel rested, but have not gotten cold. For me, that means going down to about 80 heart beats per minute. For others it may be 120 heart beats per minute.

Typical Workout: 12 x 120m with 2-3 minutes recovery between.

VO2 MAX WORKOUT

Objective: Increase maximum ability to take in and use oxygen.
Velocity: Mile race pace.
Time: Work periods of 2-6 minutes with equal periods of recovery.
Heart R: 98% to 100% of maximum.

VO_2 max is a calculus expression which literally means the amount of oxygen you can take out of the air when you are going as fast as you possibly can. As oxygen is taken from the air, it burns sugars and fats in the muscles to give you energy. These are your fuel sources.

In this workout, velocity and heart rate are probably close to 100 percent maximum. You can tolerate between 2 to 6 minutes of this exertion.

You need to include some walking at VO_2 max in your training. Be aware that this type of training is the one most likely to cause soreness or injury.

Typical Workout: 5 x 5 x 5 — five repetitions for 5 minutes with 5 minutes recovery between. You go off as fast as you can go for 5 minutes, rest and start again.

LACTATE THRESHOLD VELOCITY (LTV)

Objective: Increase lactate threshold.

Velocity: Lactate threshold velocity is about 8km race pace, but training is somewhat slower. 10 to 20 seconds per mile slower than your 10km race pace is typical.

Time: Work periods range from reps of 5 minutes to single efforts of 25 minutes. Recovery between reps is brief, permitting only the mental recovery needed to maintain technique.

Heart R. A small band of heart rates that varies between individuals, or

P.E. Perceived exertion—medium discomfort.

The purpose of training at LTV is to improve the speed at which you can walk without a rapid rise in blood lactate concentration. Several studies have shown that the faster your LTV, the faster you can race. There is even good evidence that this measure is a better predictor of race performance than is maximum oxygen uptake.

This workout is very important. When you are using oxygen to burn sugar, carbon dioxide and water are formed. When you get going fast enough, your body does not have time to do all the chemical processing. It takes a bit of sugar, which is like a ring, pulls it in half and throws the pieces away instead of turning it into carbon dioxide. These pieces float around in the blood as lactates. When you get enough concentration of them, you slow down. That concentration in the blood remains fairly constant as you go faster until you get to a certain velocity and then the curve goes up exponentially. That break point is what is called lactate threshold velocity.

Several terms have slightly different scientific definitions, but may be considered equivalent to lactate threshold velocity. These terms include: Ledge point, OBLA, Anaerobic threshold and four millimol lactate concentration.

The lactate threshold velocity is the speed you can race an 8km that causes about 4mmol of lactate to build up in the blood. It corresponds to a perceived exertion of "medium discomfort." Training for a 4mmol lactate blood concentration on a heart rate monitor is extremely effective. Unfortunately, you really need some treadmill testing with somebody sticking pins in you to ascertain your exact lactate level. For that reason, there is increasing use of perceived exertion as a monitor.

Typical Workouts: (1) A 20 to 30 minute tempo walk at a 5km race pace or **(2)** 3 x 8 minutes, 4 x 8 minutes, 3 x 10 minutes with a 1-minute recovery between. The recovery is mainly to let you mentally recover and refocus on technique. **(3)** 5 x 5 minutes with 30 seconds of recovery between. Breaking these workouts up in different ways helps make them more interesting.

In one week you need at least 25 minutes of lactate threshold work to maintain a high threshold. You need to do more than 25 minutes of training in a week to make improvements.

The figures you see for total distance or total time in the literature range from 20 minutes to 50 minutes. There is still a lot of debate about what the best amount of time is. I have found 3 x 10 minutes with 1-minute recovery between each interval works very well for me. Everyone needs to experiment because individuals differ and you need to test them on yourself.

In terms of percentage of LTV workout time a week, again, figures vary from 10 percent up to 25 percent. My answer is: If you are really going to focus on improving your lactate threshold, you need two sessions, possibly three, a week. I do not think you can tolerate more. The total amount for each of these is between 20 to 30 minutes.

You want to maximize Lactate Threshold Velocity workouts during the six weeks preceding a key race because researchers are finding that you can improve your lactate threshold by about 5 percent over a four or five week period. It also tends to fall back in a hurry so this six weeks of emphasis is important.

As with any recent scientific advance, opinions on Lactate Threshold Training abound. Some apparently contradict each other and each has its own technical vocabulary. I have tried to mix the research findings with practical experience to generate a useful guideline.

Tempo Walk: A Tempo Walk is a workout at Lactate Threshold Velocity (LTV) in which the athlete warms up and then walks at a speed 10 to 20 seconds per mile slower than his or her 10km race pace. This is a continuous effort for 20 to 30 minutes and is followed by a warm-down. If you have had a Lactate Threshold test on a treadmill, you will be able to use a target heart rate instead of a target velocity.

Bursts: Another training session at LTV could consist of a warm-up followed by 3 bursts of 8 minutes walking at 10 to 20 seconds per mile slower than your 10km race pace. A 1-minute rest is taken between efforts. This rest period is enough time to keep the walker mentally alert and able to walk with correct technique, but with most of the workout close to the target blood lactate level. As with any hard session or race, warm down at an easy pace.

AEROBIC AND EASY WALKING

The fourth and fifth training paces are brisk aerobic walking, the pace used for long workouts and easy walking. It is important to walk easy in a warm-down after a hard workout. A few days of easy walking is often wise after a maximal race effort.

The most likely way to reach your best race fitness is to carry out a sequence of several weeks of training and to focus on different training velocities. Selecting the length and order of these periods of training is a major area of scientific study at the moment.

ADDITIONAL TRAINING METHODS

PLYOMETRICS

Plyometrics is a type of training to improve the energy storage and return of the elastic tissues running within and between the muscle fibers of the leg. It is often used by hurdlers, jumpers and middle distance runners.

Examples of Plyometric exercises include hopping, bounding up hill with long slow strides, very slow running with high knee lifts, deep squat jumps and two-footed jumps off boxes with rebounding back up onto other boxes. These movements are not related to the biomechanics of racewalking, and I do not believe they will help racewalkers to race faster. There have been no scientific tests of the effect of these exercises on racewalkers.

A plyometric contraction occurs when a muscle is first stretched rapidly and then shortened to accelerate the body or a limb segment. An example of this action is a vertical jump with a prior crouching motion to store elastic energy in the thigh muscles. Vertical jump performance can be improved as much as 20 percent if the crouching motion occurs as part of the drop-jump. Several studies agree that drop-jump training increases the height of jumps preceded by a counter movement but has no important effect on jumps from a static crouch.

Kraemer and Newton summarize that plyometric drop-jump training "does not effectively increase fundamental muscular power." ("Sports Science Exchange" Vol.7 No. 6 1994) Again, I do not see a racewalking need for plyometric training that involves rapid stretching prior to contraction of any muscle groups (the exact definition of plyometric training). Racewalkers use different muscle groups and movement patterns than jumpers or runners. Moreover, these exercises may cause injury. However, I do think that such things as speed drills and dynamic weight work may be of benefit.

HEART RATE MONITORS

The heart pumps blood around the body to carry nutrients, oxygen, carbon dioxide and heat to and from exercising muscles. Each beat is a contraction of the heart's muscular wall and is caused by a tiny electric wave. A heart rate monitor is worn on the chest with an elastic strap and detects these electric changes. It calculates how many times per minute the heart is beating and transmits this information as a radio signal to a wrist watch.

Although monitors require batteries for their operation, they are perfectly safe since no electricity enters the body.

The price of monitors has dropped rapidly in the last few years and a basic model can be obtained for under $120. At the same time, accuracy and durability of the units has improved.

Heart rate is closely related to oxygen uptake and changes in blood chemistry which vary according to the amount of physical work a walker is performing. Complex lab equipment is needed to measure these factors and so heart rate is used as an easily measured approximation. Although work rate is a key factor in setting heart rate, there are great individual differences in the actual heart rates found. Factors such as age, fitness, body size, hydration and the use of hand weights will all have an effect on how fast your heart beats. Hot weather causes an upward drift in heart rate as the body tries to move heat from working muscles to the skin.

In spite of these variations, heart rate is still a better measure of work load for walkers than distance, time or speed. There are many good articles on target heart rates for fitness walking. Racewalkers often use heart rate to regulate their faster training sessions. A monitor allows the walker to continuously adjust pace to hit a target heart rate or a percentage of maximum heart rate. A heart rate monitor may be just the personal coach you need to make every step of a workout carry you towards your fitness goals.

USATF rules now specifically permit the wearing of heart rate monitors during races. If you intend to wear a monitor during a race, be aware that there are some potential problems.

- The chest strap can slip down and may require periodic adjustment.
- The chest strap may constrict breathing.
- Many devices transmit heart rates at the same radio frequency which may cause confusion if you are racing along side another athlete with a monitor.
- If worn too high, a monitor will pick up the electric output from contracting chest muscles and will give step rate instead of heart rate. (A useful trick when working on stride rate training.)
- Sweat seeping into the monitor or wrist receiver can cause bogus readings.

- The monitor may distract you from full concentration on the race or your technique.

To reduce these problems, I recommend:

- Only wear a heart rate monitor if you have a plan to use your pulse as a guide to race pace or effort.
- Just as with drinking during competition or wearing racing shoes, use your monitor often in training so that you have it adjusted for fit, and understand the relationships between the pulse reading and background interference.
- Experiment with wearing the monitor over or under your singlet to stop excess sweat entering the transmitter. Try pinning the strap to your singlet to prevent it slipping.

The monitor strap may be worn inside the front of a singlet and outside at the back, passing in and out through the arm holes. This also stops downward slipping during exercise.

TIRE DRAGGING

Dragging a tire on a flat surface is useful if you want to check if you are moving forward at a constant speed. Racewalkers slow down at heel strike and reaccelerate as the leg passes under the body. The greater the speed change through the stride, the greater the energy cost. This is similar to the effect of driving a car by pressing the accelerator and brake in rapid succession. If you have only a slight speed change through your stride, the tire will slide steadily. If the tire alternately slides and stops, it indicates a lack of smoothness in your racewalking technique.

The risk is that you will alter your technique. You will get better at dragging tires, but this is not yet an international event! There are more effective ways to improve strength such as weight training, fast intervals or racewalking up a slight hill. I suggest tire dragging as an occasional check for smooth technique but not as a strength training method.

RON LAIRD

Ron Laird, four-time Olympian and member of the Track & Field Hall of Fame, has been a longtime advocate of tire dragging. The following article lists the benefits Ron has personally found in this activity.

TIRE DRAGGING AND STRAIGHT KNEES

The best way I know to develop straight knees is to drag an old tire while racewalking. This excellent exercise also builds the pulling and pushing power of your hamstrings, calves, ankles, and toes. Your stomach and lower back will also get a good strength and flexibility workout.

Even though you move along at a slow pace, be sure to use proper technique. This is not a speed session. Starting off with a few minutes of hiking is the best way to warm up. The excess resistance of the tire will eventually, if not immediately, get your knees back where they belong.

Use a tire that is not too heavy for you and stay on level ground. My favorite place to drag it is around the outside lane of a track or on the infield. A grass surface provides very steady resistance. Clean asphalt and concrete also grip the tire well. If it slides too easily, put some weight (stones) in it.

Two or three sessions per week of 20 to 30 minutes each is a good way to start. An hour should be plenty once you have worked your way up to it. BE alert; do not strain yourself. This drill does put a lot of pressure on the hips, legs and feet.

If the tire bounces around behind you, the rope may be too short. Bouncing is also caused by uneven walking because one leg is working a little differently than the other. As soon as you equalize your hip, leg and arm efforts as well as stride length, the tire should slidc smoothly behind you. Trying to go too fast can also start it bouncing too much. Keep it smooth and let the resistance of that old tire straighten your knees back into their required legal position with each step.

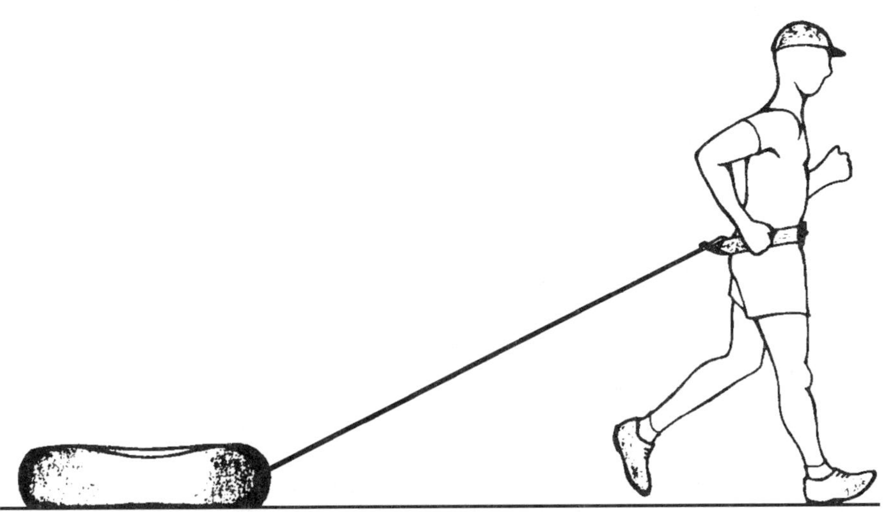

Use a strong wide belt, a couple of yards of rope, and an old tire with a small hole cut through its middle.

If you want to improve your hip turning, put the effort into twisting your hip around a little more with each step. The resistance of the tire will do the rest. As you know, good hip turning lengthens your stride and helps keep your feet down.

To develop more strength and speed, wear ankle weights. The low impact of racewalking makes them safe to use. They help build the strength used to whip your hind leg quickly away from the ground and snap it forward. Ankle weights are good training aids any time they are worn for walking and general exercising.

Another addition to this kind of training is to carry two to five pound dumbbells in your hands. These dumbbells build arm and shoulder power and endurance. Hand weights can be used during any of your walks. You will be quite a sight if you *ever* try this workout! I try to do these sessions in a secluded area.

DAVE McGOVERN

Pronounced calf and hamstring musculature will cause the back of the legs to appear bent even when the knee is fully straightened.

In my experience racewalkers suffer relatively few injuries, but nearly all are overuse injuries rather than traumatic ones.

I Creeping & Knee Straightening
II Ankle and Shin Strength
III Tendonitis

Dave McGovern is one of the sport's best and most entertaining writers. Dave holds a Bachelor of Science degree in biology and geology from the University of Rochester, a Master of Science Degree in Environmental Planning from the University of Virginia and is currently working on an MBA at La Grange College. He has been a competitive racewalker for the past twelve years and a racewalking coach for the last seven. The following essays address common problems affecting masters racewalkers.

WHAT TO DO WHEN WALKING GIVES YOU THE CREEPS
Straightening Strategies for the Frustrated Racewalker

When working with racewalkers, particularly with older racewalkers, one often encounters difficulty in helping the athlete to overcome knee-straightening problems. Although some athletes simply need to be shown the proper technique, many need to overcome more fundamental impediments before full straightening can be achieved. The unfortunate reality, however, is that very few sources actually outline procedures to conquer "creeping sickness." Much like Ross Perot's crazy aunt in the basement, everybody knows there's a problem, but nobody wants to talk about it.

ASSESSING THE PROBLEM

The first order of business is to determine if the walker is physically able to straighten the knees. Simply have the athlete stand "at attention" with feet together and legs straightened as much as possible without excessively tightening the quadriceps muscles. The fronts of the thighs and shins should make a straight line in relation to one another, or even bow inwards to meet the knee. (Be sure to examine the *front* of the legs. Pronounced calf and hamstring musculature will cause the back of the legs to appear bent even when the knee is fully straightened.)

If the legs are fully extended and the knees still look bent, tight muscles are probably to blame. After 20 to 80 years of ordinary walking as well as running, or even of advanced competitive sedentarianism, many athletes are plagued by such tight leg muscles that full straightening, even while standing, may be difficult.

GROUCHO MARX SHUFFLE

Though some athletes have no obvious muscular tightness and are able to straighten when standing, they fall into a Groucho Marx Shuffle when racewalking. These athletes need remedial work in the mechanics of racewalking. They often come from running backgrounds and are using the wrong muscles to drive themselves forward, primarily the quadriceps. Using the quads often causes a high knee lift in the leading leg which makes straightening on contact difficult.

The lead leg should be brought forward as a unit with the hip, allowing just enough knee bend for the foot to clear the ground. The large gluteal and lower back muscles rather than the quadriceps should be utilized to propel the walker forward. Many of these athletes are able to pick up proper racewalking technique by simply watching and mimicking athletes with efficient technique. Running should not be used for cross training until proper technique is fully ingrained.

STRETCHING THOSE OL' DOGS

If the creeping problem can be attributed to muscular tightness, stretching the hamstring and calf muscles may solve the problem. After warming up, the athlete should stretch the gastrocnemius and soleus muscles of the calf by performing wall stretches. The left gastrocnemius is stretched by standing with the left leg about two feet behind the right and leaning against a wall while keeping the rear heel on the ground (Figure A.) Slightly bending the knee (Figure B), will stretch the soleus. Switch legs to stretch the right calf.

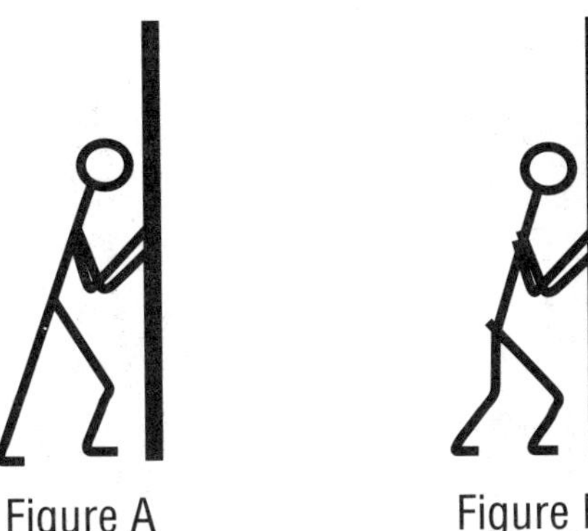

Figure A Figure B

To stretch the hamstrings, the walker should lie on his back with one knee bent, foot on the floor and the other leg extended (Figure C.) The extended leg is grasped with both hands until a stretch is felt.

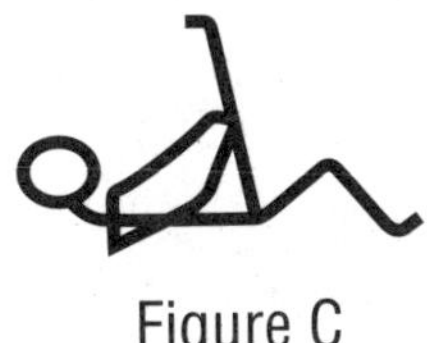

Figure C

All stretches should be held for at least 10 to 20 seconds. Athletes should stretch after every workout, but if time does not permit, at least three days per week should be devoted to an overall stretching/strengthening routine. These stretches, in addition to a proper warm-up before workouts and races, should help to reduce stiffness that may lead to bent knees.

OTHER THINGS TO TRY

- **The Brick:** Many walkers coming from running or fitness walking backgrounds have difficulty attaining a proper degree of "hip drop." Hip drop acts as a shock absorber and eases the impact of "riding through" on a straight lead leg. Without sufficient hip drop, shock is often reduced by slightly bending the knee. The specific muscles used during this phase of the walking gait can be stretched by standing with one foot on a brick or a two-by-four and the other on the floor. Of course, there is one catch. Both knees must be straightened! Always maintain a comfortable, erect posture without bending at the waist.

Figure D

Figure E

• **Strengthening:** Weak quadriceps muscles are another contributor to bent knees. The quadriceps (the muscles in front of the thighs) can be strengthened at home with a "dynaband" or other elastic device, or with a light (10 lb.) weight hung from the ankle. A simple implement can be made by inserting a pair of small five pound weights into a long sock. After tying off the end of the sock, the device can be hung from the ankle with one weight hanging on each side of the leg.

The athlete should sit in a sturdy chair with one leg fully extended. The knee is then bent 15 to 20 degrees, then restraightened to lift the weight. Work up to three sets of ten repetitions to strengthen the quadriceps through the final 15 to 20 degrees of their range of motion.

• **Fat Shoes:** Avoid wearing "fat" shoes. If the athlete is walking flatfooted, lifting the forefoot slightly upon heel contact will help to straighten the knee by slightly extending the reach of the lower leg. Shin pain, however, may prevent walking with the toes raised. At the moment of heel contact a walker's shoe acts like a lever. The thicker the midsole, the greater the force imparted to the heel extending behind the ankle, the fulcrum of the lever. If the walker wears a shoe with a very thick heel, the foot tends to flatten quickly, slapping the ground with every step. This often causes pain in the anterior tibialis or shin muscles. Wearing a thinner shoe will reduce these forces and ultimately ease knee straightening. Strengthening the ankle and shin muscles are also important. Again, a dynaband, or a hanging sock with lighter weights, can be used. Walking for several minutes on the heels is another excellent strengthening exercise.

• **Avoid Overstriding:** When the advancing leg is thrown too far forward, the knee will often reflexively "break" to make heel contact with the ground sooner. Of course, this may prevent the walker from falling on his face, but it can lead to a far worse fate — disqualification. Shortening the stride in front of the body will not only eliminate straightening problems in some individuals, it will also increase efficiency. "Riding" on the straight leg far beyond the vertical support phase by keeping the rear foot on the ground longer will make up for lost stride length in front of the body and increase power.

• **Posture, Posture, Posture:** (Figure F) Body posture is also very important. Many racewalkers tend to slump forward by bending excessively at the waist. The center of gravity is shifted forward over the lead leg. When walking speed is increased, momentum collapses the knee when the heel touches the ground.

Lean From the Ankles

Don't Bend at the Waist

Figure F

A forward lean of 5 to 8 degrees is recommended to aid quick turnover and strong propulsion from the rear leg, but this lean must come from the ankle, not the waist. Body carriage must be erect despite the overall forward lean.

- **Hill Work:** Racewalking slowly up a gradual incline is an excellent way to accentuate proper straightening technique. Forward lean, a short stride in front of the body and a strong drive from the rear leg are all necessary when racewalking up hills. The athlete should walk several repeats up the hill under supervision of a knowledgeable friend or spouse. Hills tend to magnify technique problems especially when the athlete is fatigued. The partner should make certain that the athlete is walking correctly at all times.

After objectively assessing the reasons behind a particular walker's creeping tendencies, it is often relatively easy to eliminate the problem. If the athlete's technique is a hybrid of running and walking elements, flaws can be eliminated by a demonstration of the proper technique. If tightness and weakness are to blame, the walker must thoroughly stretch and strengthen the affected areas. Patience and persistence are generally rewarded by better, faster and more legal racewalk technique.

THE IMPORTANCE OF ANKLE AND SHIN STRENGTH

Nearly every beginning racewalker has experienced the intense burning in the shins that signals the full awakening of the anterior tibialis muscles. These muscles are rarely, if ever, fully activated in any other sport but racewalking, so such pain is not surprising. Novice racewalkers are also frequently frustrated by an inefficient, "stumpy" walking style that prevents them from competing with comparably fit, but more economical athletes.

Despite the emphasis many walking coaches and athletes put on hands, arms, elbows and even noses (!), the feet are the only parts of the body that are in contact with the ground during the walking gait. They play a vital role both in providing propulsive force and in allowing this force to be transferred into forward momentum. This article will describe how strengthening the muscles of the foot and lower leg can help to eliminate shin pain and improve walking efficiency, legality and speed.

THE SWING VS PROPULSIVE PHASES OF WALKING

The stride of a racewalker in motion can be logically broken down into two distinct, albeit intimately connected, phases. These are the so-called "swing" and "propulsive" phases.

The swing phase begins as soon as the rear foot loses contact with the ground. The knee of the rear leg bends to allow the advancing foot to clear the ground as it comes forward. The momentum of the leg's mass swinging forward causes the walker's body to fall forward and to pivot about the supporting foot of the other leg.

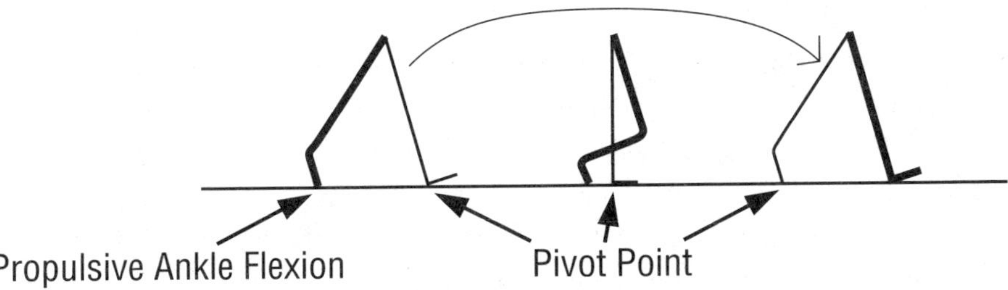

The propulsive phase, which occurs concurrently with the swing phase, begins as soon as the advancing foot contacts the ground in front of the body. As the heel is "planted," the gluteal muscles contract, helping the body to pivot over the leg. After the body's center of gravity passes over the supporting foot, the calf muscles contract and the ankle flexes as the foot pushes down into the ground.

This action provides a strong propulsive force that helps to move the body forward. Pushing off strongly from the rear in this manner allows for a momentary lag in the stride cycle which causes the opposite side of the hip to swing forward. This extends the walker's effective stride length, and helps to align the feet, one in front of the other. The explosive push-off also helps to initiate a strong swing phase of the next stride.

REMOVING BARRIERS TO SPEED

In addition to necessitating the generation of a great deal of explosive power, high-speed racewalking requires that the athlete remove any barriers that may prevent this power from being translated into forward motion. There is no single optimum race walking style. Each walker does the best he or she can given the constraints of level of conditioning, body type and degree of muscular flexibility. Consequently, video analysis shows that different racewalkers can utilize a variety of different swing-to-propulsion phase ratios in their stride cycles. For example, some walkers tend to generate more power via a strong swing phase while others benefit from a strong, propulsive ankle flexion.

Although different coaches may favor one approach over another, all walkers can benefit from improving ankle strength and flexibility because strong foot action is required during <u>all</u> phases of the walking gait.

A. Heel Plant: Racewalkers must possess sufficient shin strength to hold the toes up during heel plant, otherwise the foot will flatten out due to strong levering forces acting on the heel. If the shins are too weak to hold the toes up, the flattened foot acts a lot like the broad base of a floor lamp. The base imparts stability to the lamp and prevents it from toppling over, but stability is the last thing a walker needs. The walker actually wants to fall forward, pivoting around the small contact point that the outer edge of the heel provides.

A flattened foot creates a braking effect that brings a momentary interruption in forward momentum. This braking effect tends to cause a very percussive, jolting stride as the foot hits the ground with excessive downward force. A great deal of this force is transferred directly to the knee and can cause a less than solidly locked knee to collapse. Many older walkers have been able to cure this kind of creeping problem by simply strengthening the shin muscles.

B. Single Support Phase: After heel contact the walker should roll smoothly on the outer edge of the shoe until the body passes directly over the foot. The foot should not flop down before this point. If the foot does flatten out prematurely, braking forces will again interrupt forward momentum. Strong ankle and peroneal muscles will prevent the foot from collapsing too soon and allow a fluid, efficient rolling motion.

C. Toe Off: Once the road blocks have been removed, a racewalker can utilize his foot, ankle and lower calf muscles to generate forward momentum. The walker should begin flexing the calf muscles as soon as the body passes directly over the foot and continue until the toes push off the ground far behind the body. To maximize propulsive power, the foot should roll completely up to the toes. Many walkers begin the swing phase too early, punching the knee forward while the ball of the foot is still on the ground. Early retraction is counterproductive because power is dissipated as soon as the knee begins to collapse. Always strive to fully flex the ankle behind the body while the rear leg is still straight to maximize the effect of the propulsive phase.

PUMP UP THOSE TIRES!

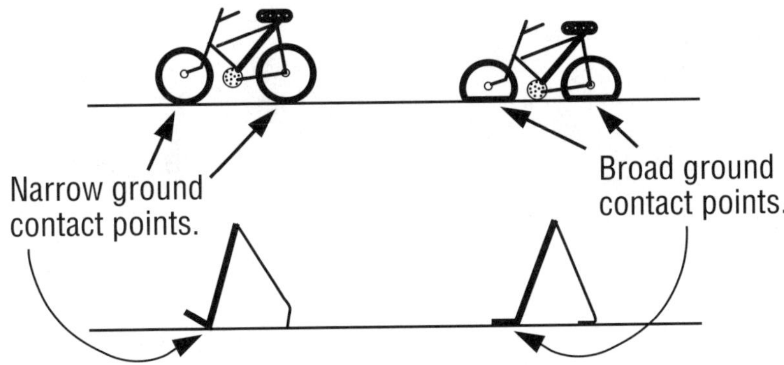

Strong shins and ankles throughout the foot's entire range of motion allow the body to pivot very smoothly over the ankle joint, much like a bicycle tire rolling about the axis of its hub. Racewalking without sufficient shin and ankle strength is like trying to ride a bicycle with two very flat tires. You can, but you cannot "roll" forward very smoothly.

Shin and ankle strength is imperative to effectively maintain proper foot placement throughout the stride cycle. How can a walker strengthen these muscles?

- Walk on your heels with straight knees to strengthen shin muscles. Continue for about 30 seconds, stretch and repeat.

- Perform toe raises for shin strength and calf raises for calf and ankle strength. Stand on the edge of a step with the front three-quarters of the foot hanging over the edge. Slowly dip the feet down, then all the way up. Repeat until fatigue is felt in the shin. Stretch and repeat several times. For calves and ankles stand on a step with the back three-quarters of the foot hanging off the step. Dip up and down, stretch and repeat as above.
- To strengthen the bottoms of the feet use toe grip exercises. Repeatedly pick up a towel or other soft object with your foot by curling your toes.
- Racewalk slowly up a gradual incline to strengthen the ankles and calves. Hill work will also help to ingrain proper heel placement. Somewhat faster hill repeats may be used to develop an explosive toe-off.
- Specific range of motion exercises with some form of elastic band or tubing are excellent for isolating weak areas of the shins and ankles. Simply loop a heavy elastic band around the foot and work the muscles against the resistance provided by the elastic.
- Avoid "fat" shoes. The thicker the midsole, the greater the levering force imparted to the heel. Shoes or running flats with a low heel will help to keep the foot from flattening prematurely.

To reduce "stumpiness," your feet must be a strong, active part of the walking motion. Racewalking will eventually strengthen the feet and lower leg muscles, but by adding some of these extra exercises to your daily routine you will be able to drastically reduce the time required to build up these muscles. Reduced shin pain and more efficient, legal walking technique may be just a couple of feet away!

TENDONITIS AND BURSITIS

(The following is an excerpt from Dave's essay on a bout of knee tendonitis he had after racing in the New York Marathon.)

In my experience racewalkers suffer relatively few injuries, but nearly all are overuse injuries rather than traumatic ones (i.e. sprains and tears). Common racewalking injuries are: Knee tendonitis (iliotibial or sartorial), feet (plantar fascitis or cuboid peroneal syndrome), shins (shin splints or posterior tibial myositis/tendonitis) and Achilles tendonitis. Bursitis of the hip or knee is also fairly common.

The trick with tendonitis is to remember just what tendons are. Tendons are tough fibrous sheaths that connect muscles to bones. Fortunately, 99 percent of the time there is nothing wrong with the tendon itself. It is simply being abused by a tight muscle.

Racewalking, like running, does nothing to enhance flexibility. The racewalker is propelled forward by *contracting* muscles. Over time, the muscles incrementally lose flexibility if they are not stretched gently after exercise. As a tight muscle shortens, it pulls at its origin and at its insertion point (at the tendons and fascial sheaths). The only way to release the strain on the tendon is to stretch the muscle.

Similarly, bursitis is the inflammation of a bursa (a fluid-filled sac) found or formed in areas of friction. As the muscles tighten, friction around the joints increases and bursae are irritated. Releasing tight muscles reduces friction and allows the bursa to return to normal.

REMEDIES:

We are often ingrained with a quick-fix, Band-Aid approach to sports medicine. We are told rest, ice and aspirin will make the pain go away. All true, but these approaches attack the symptom and not the cause. The pain is in a tendon or bursa, but the root cause is the tight, neglected muscle.

Treatment for these injuries must begin with isolation of the muscle or muscles involved. In most cases the athlete will notice discomfort and tightness in a certain muscle that may lie far from the injured area. Do not ignore these sensations!

My last serious bout with tendonitis involved the insertion of my iliotibial band into the outside of my right knee. I felt a little tight on the outside of my right hip as well, but thought nothing of it since it was never very painful. Meanwhile two months of rest did nothing to cure the knee once I tried to return to training. I was in exactly the same stage of pain after two months of rest because I failed to attack the tight iliotibial band and hip muscles.

The treatment that finally cured me involved deep manipulation of the scar tissue in my hip and thigh to release the muscle and tendon. I also learned how to ward off further flare-ups with a sensible stretching routine.

OUNCE OF PREVENTION

An ounce of prevention is worth two in the bush (or something like that.) If the weather is just too lousy to get out the door to train, stay inside and stretch! Attack those tight muscles before they turn into debilitating injuries. There are dozens of excellent books out there on stretching. Perhaps Bob Anderson's *Stretching* is the best known, but each individual must find the particular stretches that work for him or her. Experiment to see which positions get it right where it hurts. Certainly stretching is an important first step in recovery, but gains in flexibility will be short-lived if the involved muscles are weak and atrophied.

Strength training is equally critical in injury rehabilitation or preventative care. Whether using free weights, weight machines, elastic devices or isometric exercises, the involved muscles should be isolated in such a way as to ensure that they are being worked through a range of motion that mimics their racewalking action as closely as possible. This may involve a good deal of improvisation with weight machines, or experimentation with postural changes until the best position is found.

Do not ignore those minor aches and pains. Head off injuries at the pass by listening to your body. Stretch and strengthen problem areas as needed before they blow up on you. Got it? Great! Now just do it. Then, get out there and walk!

RICHARD CHARLES

Water workouts can be similar to those on a track — interval training, fartlek, ladders or hurdles.

Body awareness develops by focusing on specific parts of the body when you are working out in the water or on land.

I Deep Water Training
Benefits
How To's
Workouts
Rehabilitation After Injury.

Richard Charles, Racewalk Chair of the Southern Texas Association, is a certified exercise instructor for those who are "chronologically superior." He lives in Austin, Texas, where he promotes deep water walking as a method of cross-training. Because Bev LaVeck, Ray Funkhouser and other highly successful masters athletes and coaches have used or are using deep water walking in their training programs, its merits are worth exploring.

DEEP WATER TRAINING

BENEFITS

From the racewalking point of view, deep water walking develops the front and back muscles of the legs and arms, works the hip flexors and improves range of motion. In fact, it benefits all muscle groups. By stretching and strengthening the major muscle groups, it can lead to improved stride length and improved P.R.'s.

You will have a lower heart rate working out in water than you will with a similar workout on land. Specifically, your workout heart rate is about 10 to 15 beats slower in water than on the land. A reason for the slower heart rate is that the water pressure massages your body as you move in the water and assists the blood's return to the heart. Also, circulation is aided by the near zero gravity environment.

Another valuable aspect of a water workout is that by your own energy and effort you can develop anywhere from 5 to 40 times more resistance in water than in air. The amount depends on how fast you try to move your arms and legs. The average water resistance is 12 to 14 times greater than that encountered on land. A hard 30 minute workout in water equates with a 45 minute workout on land, and you can gain this intensity without pain.

THE HOW-TO'S

When you are doing deep water walking, you have to have access to water deep enough so that you can be in a spinal neutral position. Water that is as deep as you are tall works well; however, optimum workouts are accomplished in depths above your head. Lap pools with waist deep water present a different challenge that can be met with imagination.

I work out at a local "Y" in a regulation pool with lanes. The diving end has a 20-foot segment that tapers down. Using a lane, I work as hard as I can in one direction, then turn and go in the other direction. The point is that when you are walking or running in water, forward movement is not important. The important element is time. The pool at the "Y" has competition clocks at both ends so I can keep tabs on whether I have done 30 seconds or 60 seconds of effort during an interval workout.

With deep water training, you use a flotation device that keeps the water level just below your chin. As you are in a spinal neutral position, you can completely relax and will have maximum spacing between your vertebrae. Because you are not concerned about trying to keep afloat, you can really concentrate on the movements of driving your legs forward and moving your arms.

My preferred flotation devise is a WET VEST™ jacket. These units have front and back panels integrated in wet suit material. Hook fasteners (Velcro) provide infinite adjustments for a comfortable fit. Waist belts are available under trade names SPEEDO™, AQUAJOGGER™, WET BELT™. All belts tend to migrate forward. The WET BELT™ is more form fitting. Before making any purchase try out the different equipment.

WORKOUTS

Again, forward movement is not important when walking or running in water. Focus on technique. Keep your abdominal muscles firm, squeeze those glutes (butt), and tip your pelvis forward. Maintain a forward lean from the ankles not the waist! If your abdominals and glutes are contracted, your back will be flat.

Much cardiovascular training today is done using heart rate POLAR™ monitors. These monitors record underwater and transmit heart rates to a wrist watch. With a monitor, you can observe instantaneous readings to grade your efforts.

After training a while in deep water, you can learn to monitor your body and judge your effort of exertion. The method in general use today is the modified BORG Scale of Perceived Exertion (0-no effort, 10= maximum effort), or more simply, how you feel as you are working out. If I ask a student, "How are you doing?" and I can barely make out an answer through the panting, I tell him or her to ease off.

Water workouts can be similar to those on a track — interval training, fartlek, ladders or hurdles. An example of a water interval workout would be: Walk or run all out for 30 seconds, walk slowly in the water to recover for 30 seconds and go another 30 seconds all out. When you do a ladder workout, you start out at a reduced effort and gradually increase the intensity.

Being coached from the pool deck can help you maintain proper technique. An underwater video taken of you training will give the appearance that you are walking (or running) on an invisible glass surface.

Deep water walking two or three times a week for three months will bring noticeable improvements in flexibility. I do not confine workouts in the water just to walking. I will run in the water. I will visualize myself going over hurdles — extending the lead foot and bringing the other leg up with the opposite arm's elbow reaching out until it almost breaks the surface of the water. I will use my body in all sorts of ways to involve new muscle patterns.

Listen to your body! Warm up muscles before increasing intensity (water resistance). A workout may leave you feeling pleasantly tired, but you will not hurt yourself. Be sensible, you will know when you are working too hard. If so, ease off.

Do not follow a water workout with a land workout. Your limbs will feel like lead. The reverse is fine. After you have had a good land workout, getting into a pool and easing along in the water will relax and stretch your muscles. Follow this with pool side stretching. Allow yourself 15 minutes to relax and stretch your muscles.

REHABILITATION AFTER INJURY

If you are under the care of a physician or other health care professional, pay attention to the advice that is given. Water workouts have proven to be most beneficial, but be sure that you have thoroughly discussed this medium of exercise with him or her.

People frequently think of water in terms of rehabilitation. Because of its unique properties and the intense exercise it allows, athletes can build up strength in their injured part while maintaining their aerobic conditioning. At the same time, deep water workouts are excellent cross-training for athletes who are in good condition and want to improve their overall body mobility and strength.

Working in water will also reveal muscle imbalance. For example, when an athlete starts moving around in the water, I watch to see if he or she tends to favor one side over the other. Many times when people begin working quite hard, you will see them start turning in the water because one leg or arm is stronger than its opposite. Asymmetry immediately signals that a person needs to do drills to develop the weaker side. It is a very simple test of technique and range of motion.

You learn body awareness by learning to focus. When I have students in the water, I have them concentrate on their leg movements, on driving their hips forward and on their arms moving in the water. Body awareness develops by focusing on specific parts of the body when you are working out in the water or on land.

When I work with masters, I am especially concerned about increasing range of motion and body strength. By walking or running in the water, masters get a total workout. In contrast, swimming is about 80 percent upper body and running is about 80 percent lower body. However, as far as maintaining or improving bone density, a person has to workout on land.

Right now, those over 65 form about seven percent of the population. In 2000, they will be about eleven percent and in 2020, about twenty percent. Exercise is proving extremely important to enjoying a quality life all the way. I am 72-years-old now. If you use the guide of losing one beat from your maximal heart rate each year, I have 128 beats left. I told my wife that I am not checking out until I run out of beats. Her response, "That's a scary thought."

Shirley Capps

Jack Bray

SHIRLEY CAPPS (W55)
JACK BRAY (M60)

SHIRLEY CAPPS

Two of the most important elements for racewalking are flexibility for technique and relaxation for training and racing.

The times that I did not put off trying something new, or did not wait for someone else to go with me, changed my life. They led me down so many paths and opened so many wonderful doors.

I Relaxation & Flexibility
Kundalini Yoga and T'ai Chi
15 Chinese exercises for warm up
II Pilates and the Personal Performer™
III Popular forms of Fitness Equipment
IV Shallow Water Aerobics
V Massage Roller

Shirley Capps (W55) won gold medals at the Masters Outdoor Championships in Provo, Utah, in 1993 - 5km 32:30 and 10km 1:07:55. In Eugene, Oregon, 1994, she placed 5th in the 5km with a time of 31:23.0, and 4th in the 10km with a time of 64:23. A former registered nurse, Shirley has become knowledgeable in most of the popular supplemental forms of fitness training. In the following, she address various forms of stretching and strengthening modalities.

RELAXATION & FLEXIBILITY

KUNDALINI YOGA AND T'AI CHI

I am very tight and always have been. When I started racewalking, I started to take exercise classes to gain some flexibility. In my first class I learned how to relax as well as how to stretch. The instructor always played relaxation tapes for us as we were stretching to involve both the mind and body in the process. This combination is very helpful for people who are tight or tense.

The next class I took was in Kundalini Yoga. Again, the emphasis was on the total integration of mind and body. Yoga and similar disciplines teach if you can relax your mind, your body will relax; or if you can relax your body, your mind will relax. It does not always happen. The tensions and problems you bring to class may interfere, but when you truly are able to relax, you feel completely in tune with your body.

In yoga, I learned that my stiffness came primarily from tension, and now that I have arthritis as many people do, the tension can cause pain. Since learning yoga, I really focus on relaxing whenever my body hurts. When I have had a painful day and come to racewalking class, if I am able to relax and get everything moving, I will feel better than I have all day.

After taking yoga for a period of time, I became involved with T'ai chi. I still do the Chinese flexibility exercises used for warming up. The exercises are usually done 36 times in each direction. There is no known reason for the number 36. It probably goes back to some ancient warrior.

CHINESE EXERCISES FOR WARM-UP

FIVE ROTATIONS

- **Neck Rotations:** With your feet together, you place your hands on your waist. Rotate your neck slowly 36 times clockwise and 36 times counterclockwise.
- **Torso Rotations:** With your feet together, place your hands on your back with thumbs pointing to the ground. Rotate your torso 36 times each direction with minimal hip rotation.
- **Hip Rotations:** Feet apart, place your hands on the sides of your hips. Keeping your knees straight, rotate your hips 36 times each direction.
- **Knee Rotations:** Feet together, place your hands on your knees. Rotate your knees 12 times clockwise and stop. Press your knees back firmly a few times and then rotate your knees 12 times counterclockwise. Do three sets.

• **Arm Rotations:** In a semi lunge position, place your right hand on your front bent knee with your other leg extended behind you. Rotate your left arm in a vertical circle 18 times in both direction. Reverse your stance and rotate your right arm.

FIVE STRETCHES

• **Finger Stretching:** Lock your fingers together with palms facing out. Circle your arms out and in toward your body 36 times with your fingers stretched.

• **Toe Touching:** Feet together and with fingers locked, bend forward 36 times without bending your knees. (You may chose to do this one with slightly bent knees if you have a lower back problem.) Keep your back straight and your head facing front. When you can reach your toes with ease, fold your arms and try to reach your toes with your forearms.

• **Side Stretching:** Feet together and fingers locked over your head, palms out, bend your body from side to side 36 times gently.

• **Front Stretching:** Place one foot out in front with your knee straight and your toes pointing up in the air. Bend your supporting leg keeping both knees close together. Lower your head and stretch slowly toward your toes with your body straight. Do 15 times on each side.

• **Side Squatting:** Feet apart and toes pointing toward the front, shift your body to one side and lower your body by bending one knee. Keep the other leg straight and your body in an upright position. Place one hand on your bent knee and reach with the other hand toward your toes. Count 18 and do other side.

LEG EXERCISES

• **Leg Kicking-1:** Feet together and hand on your back with thumbs pointing to the front. Alternate kicking with your legs in the opposite directions. (Left leg kicks to the right, and right to the left.) Keep your knee locked when you kick and your toes pointing up, toward you.

• **Leg Kicking-2:** Same as above except flex your knee when you kick.

• **Squatting:** Squat with both feet firmly planted on the ground and hold for one minute.

• **Knee Raises:** Raise one knee and hold it firmly to your chest while keeping your body straight and maintaining good balance. Pull your toe inward with the other hand until it touches your thigh. Hold this posture for 1 minute. Repeat on the other side.

- **Forward bend on one leg:** Bend your knee and bring your foot to your buttocks. Hold on to your instep with your hand. Maintain balance on one leg without bending your supporting knee. Bend your body forward and try to reach your toe with your hand. Hold this posture for 30 seconds. Repeat on the other side.

Another very helpful aspect of T'ai chi involves learning to feel the tension in your body. When you try to do a movement the way the instructors request, they will immediately observe your tension areas. You think you are relaxed and then an instructor comes up and taps you on a part of your body that has not relaxed. It may be your hands, your face or your whole posture. If you have any imbalances or weaknesses, they reveal themselves because you do all the movements on both sides. By focusing your mind and body on relaxing and/or moving the problem area symmetrically, you can gradually feel improvement.

When I talk about relaxing the mind in yoga or T'ai chi, the process is similar to meditation. Everybody has their own way of defining meditation, but I am talking about relaxing the mind so that you become totally aware of what is happening in your body.

I never had body awareness until I started taking classes to develop flexibility. When someone told me that I was tight in the shoulders, I was not aware of the tightness. I could not feel if one shoulder was higher than the other, or if my head was tilted to the right. Many of us develop lifelong habits of ignoring uncomfortable or painful body sensations and make compensations that themselves cause problems.

A lot of us who are coming into racewalking are coming in at an older age. I was 53 when I started and up to then had been busy with family and work. I had not had the opportunity to be in athletics. The children who are participating in sports today are much more aware of their bodies. There is so much more information. When I started taking classes, I just could not get enough because it helped me understand how to deal with the stiffness and pain I was experiencing.

I took one fitness and stretching class several times because the teacher was so empathic. She always included reading and writing assignments each semester. I actually learned how to write better, because I wrote from my heart about all the feelings and changes I was experiencing. The words just flowed. I found it very helpful, not only physically, but mentally.

PILATES & THE PERSONAL PERFORMER™

If there was only one piece of equipment I could have for fitness, it would be a Pilates machine. Pilates was developed by a man named Joseph Pilates. He had many physical limitations and invented a set of pulleys to help him overcome them. His first machine has since been refined into one called the Personal Performer™. This particular machine is used by the Physical Therapy Unit of St. Francis Hospital in San Francisco. The machine comes with a program called "Fit and Flexible Exercises."

The exercises are not for aerobic conditioning, but for balanced strength and flexibility conditioning. For example, the equipment aligns and supports your back and neck while exercising. In addition, most of the exercises are non-impact or low-impact, and many are non-weight-bearing.

Because of its safety factor, Pilates is good for rehabilitating after an injury. Not surprisingly, the exercises are good for injury prevention, too. The exercises assist you in becoming strong, flexible and balanced at the same time.

I became interested in Pilates for improving my racewalking performances. Many machines take the "body parts" approach to conditioning and involve isolated exercises for each muscle group. Pilates trains the whole body, coordinating the upper and lower musculature with the body's center. Most exercises on the Personal Performer™ work many muscle groups at once in smooth, continuous movements.

The goal is a balanced, well-conditioned body. As with yoga, T'ai chi and other similar disciplines, the inventor of Pilates believed that it is the mind that builds the body. By concentrating on proper alignment, correct breathing and smoothness of motion, you get "in tune" with your body. I have found it quite relaxing and energizing.

Pilates is for all fitness levels. I think I am typical of most men and women as they get older. There is a natural process of tightening that occurs, and gaining and maintaining flexibility is of great importance.

I have bought many different kinds of exercise equipment over the years. I have a stair-stepper, a stationary bicycle and a Nordic Track. I have used a rowing machine. They all offer aerobic benefits and some strength training, but they do not develop flexibility or range of motion specifically. It is possible to overtrain some muscles and undertrain others on these machines which creates muscle imbalances and joint strains that may lead to injury.

Light weight training is particularly popular today. But again, free weights or weight machines train strength, but not flexibility and coordination. Pilates does both. The Pilates machine aids flexibility by taking you through your whole range of motion. You can do the prescribed exercises either lying down, kneeling or sitting. It aids strength as you can adjust the tension of the pulleys. If you are doing an exercise for your arm abductors, you use a very light tension to avoid straining them. If you are working your quads or hamstrings, you can use greater tension.

One Pilates routine I really like involves the neck. Certain stretches on the Personal Performer™ allow me to adjust my neck on one side. I need my chiropractor for the other side, but when I found I could help myself, I was really excited.

A video comes with the machine which offers excellent information. The video instructor always reminds you to keep your abdominals concave which means keeping them pulled up and in. She always reminds you to be aware of your body position and to keep your pelvis horizontal and aligned.

Pilates instructors suggest that you use other disciplines for aerobic conditioning, and I love my Nordic Track. I have a tendency to want to do everything I learn. I do not substitute. I keep adding new ways of exercising and that can get me in a lot of trouble. My body starts sending "stop" messages. Right now, I swim, do water aerobics, use the Pilates machine and my Nordic Track as supplements to my racewalking.

SHALLOW WATER AEROBICS

In my water aerobics class all the exercises are done in the shallow end of the pool so you are on your feet. The instructors want you to have your feet down. At one point, they encourage you to tread water for a minute to get the heart rate up, but if you cannot do it, you can hold on to the side of the pool and work your body hard.

We do leg work — kicks to the front, side and back; marching; jogging and knee lifts. There is a lot of arm work. There is jumping up in the air and shooting baskets through imaginary hoops. You feel like a fish because it does not hurt in your muscles. You jump way up and it does not jar you when you land. I feel like a child in that class and just love it.

I was afraid to attend a class for a long time and put it off. Then I finally made myself go. Now I kick myself because I did not go sooner. Everyone is very supportive.

MASSAGE ROLLER

There is another piece of equipment I would like to mention which is good for massaging tense, painful areas of the body. Of course, you have your own hands, but you can get weary of massaging yourself. The massaging device I have in mind is an ethafoam roller. It is made of hard, dense foam and the rollers come in 6-inch, 4-inch and 3-inch diameter cylinders. By lying on a roller, you can "unfold" or "open up" and stretch in ways that are not possible with traditional methods. This is possible because gravity assists you when you are on the roller. You just lie down and do simple movements.

Specifically, the roller allows you to stretch your chest, rib cage and pelvis to gain more freedom of movement. It also gently spreads and separates your muscle fibers, increasing blood flow and loosening restrictions.

The inventor, Ralph Havens is a physical therapist in San Diego specializing in spinal rehabilitation. He gives exercises for massaging such racewalk specific areas as the quads, hams, glutes, hips, shoulders and arms. He says that the roller exercises correct muscular imbalances and faulty patterns of movement.

The thing I like the most is that you can evaluate which parts of your body need work, do a few minutes of exercises on the roller, and then reevaluate for changes. The exercises are basically easy and fun to perform, and you can do them as often as you like. They give a deep massage which reaches painful pressure points.

CONCLUSION

I understand the needs of the older person coming into masters racewalking who needs to limber up. Pilates may not be an option for everyone because the machine is not cheap. If a man or woman enjoys being in the water, swimming and water aerobics are excellent. T'ai chi and yoga are excellent, too. These activities are readily available, and they teach body awareness, relaxation and flexibility. T'ai chi is especially good for balance. You also meet many nice people.

The first hard step is just doing something new. Trying any new activity involves the risk of doing something different and unknown. When you do something new, however, you usually discover how much you benefit and want to kick yourself for holding back. The times I did not put off trying something new, or did not wait for someone else to go with me, changed my life. They led me down so many paths and opened so many wonderful doors. It has been a good journey psychologically, mentally and physically. (See Appendix for information on Pilates machine and massage roller.)

JACK BRAY (M60)

As a master racewalker, I need all my internal energy. Relaxing and reducing stress allows energy to flow.

Since 90 percent of a race is won by your mental attitude, just keep focused on doing the best race you can.

I Chi Kung & Tao Body Scan
II A Positive Attitude

Jack Bray won the gold in both Senior Olympic Events in 1994 and 1995. In 1994, he was national champion in the 5km 26:34 and 20km 1:55:37. In 1995 he was silver medalist in the 5km 25:43. He was the M55 and M60 5km world champion at the World Veterans Games in Miyazaki, Japan, 1993 with a time of 25:09, and in Buffalo, New York, 1995 with a time of 25:10. President and coach of the Marin Race Walkers, Jack teaches walking as the dance of life. His warm up and cool down exercises come from the disciplines of T'ai chi and Chi Kung.

CHI KUNG

Flexibility and a workable technique come first. Flexibility is perhaps the hardest to attain and essential to good technique. I am constantly working on flexibility as I have a tendency to be stiff.

I do the special exercises of Chi Kung. These exercises are 1000 years old and come from China. My wife and I teach Chi Kung. It involves very subtle breathing and the manipulation of Chi energy throughout your body. It heightens body awareness.

For example, when I am warming up for a race, I take my hands, rub them together and rub them over the areas of my body which are not as flexible and supple as I want them to be. It brings Chi energy to these areas to relax muscle tightness and heal pain.

From the Tao point of view, I practice and teach the inner smile. The inner smile is a relaxation technique. You start by smiling from your eyes, behind your eyes, dropping the smile to your lips, down to your heart, and through the internal organs. This relaxes your body parts and energizes you for the race ahead. As a master racewalker, I need all my internal energy. By reducing stress, the inner smile allows energy to flow.

You may have heard Frank Alongi say, "Smile," when he is coaching. Smiling relaxes the face and body. When you are competing, try transmitting an inner smile from your eyes down through your body and see if it does not relax and energize you at the same time.

I also use the Taoist body scan. When you are waiting to start a race and feel a little tense, or are in the process of racing and begin to fall behind, scan yourself from the top of your head down your neck to your shoulders, arms, hands, chest, stomach, hips, thighs, hamstrings, calves, shins, ankles and feet. Work that visualization through your body and find out what muscles are tense or tight. As you come to a tight area, stop the scan and work on relaxing and loosening the tightness. Then start scanning again.

A POSITIVE ATTITUDE

To participate fully in the physical activity of racewalking, you need to cultivate more awareness of the intersecting paths of your body, mind and spirit. Awareness of your body's messages can help you develop more energy. For example, you may need to rest more, or you may need to take a yoga or T'ai chi class to learn how to be less stiff and rigid. Anything that you can do to train yourself to listen to your body, mind and spirit in new and exciting ways will help you improve your racing performance.

A positive attitude can also greatly increase available energy. The will to become better enables you to contact deeper levels of understanding. In *Thinking Body, Dancing Mind**, Huang and Lynch suggest the follow guides for continual self improvement.

- Stress. To experience breakthroughs, you need to extend a bit beyond your normal comfort zone.
- Rest. Many athletes are quick to stress but fail to rest.
- Stretch. Failure to stretch creates stiffness, soreness, tightness and leads to injury. Stretching becomes even more crucial as we age.

- Consistency. Improvement in anything is a direct result of how consistently you engage in the activity. It is better to workout for 30 minutes four times a week than two hours one day a week.
- Gradualness. The journey to continual self-improvement is a slow one. Be patient and persistent, and celebrate small strides.
- Emptiness. Establish an attitude of openness to new and better ways. When you think you have all the answers, you will not see other ways. See yourself as an empty vase, ready and willing to take in all that may help you to improve.

I am still learning and refining my racewalking technique. I do not know what my limits are. With major races each year, I have sufficient motivation to keep training. I always race for fun and to be a role model. I believe that the athletic life is a fountain of youth. I want other masters to share what Max Green and I share. We spur each other on to greater heights through positive competition.

I tell the masters in my club, "Do not beat yourselves up if you cannot get out and train as much as you would like. Quality not quantity workouts make for the most effective training."

Most of us learn that one of the best rewards in training and racing is that exercise makes you feel better. There is no need to think about slowing down as the years go by. Since 90 percent of a race is won by your mental attitude, the trick is to keep focused on doing the best race you can. Everyone is a winner who finishes a race with a feeling of enjoyment and accomplishment.

*Chungliang Al Huang & Jerry Lynch, *Thinking Body, Dancing Mind, Taosports for Extraordinary Performance in Athletics, Business and Life* (New York, Bantum Books, 1992), p.231-3.

BERNIE FINCH, D.C.

COMMON INJURIES

CAUSES OF INJURY

Muscle and skeletal imbalances.
Overuse, overstress, overracing.
Metabolic illnesses like flu and colds.
Muscle tears that heal with scar tissue.

INJURY PREVENTION

Balanced training, rest and nutrition.
Care of small injuries.
Careful rehabilitation of major injuries.
Avoidance of cause of injury.

I Stress
II Hamstring Injuries
III Anterior Compartment (Shin Muscles)
III Hiatal Hernia
IV Lower Back

Bernie Finch is a chiropractor in Pepin, Wisconsin. He has participated as a racewalker in 12 World Veteran's Championships. He is a four time gold medalist in the National 3Km, 5Km, 20Km and 1-Hour Championships and a five time silver medalist in the National 50Km Championship. In addition, he is six time silver medalist in the national 3km steeplechase. AAU Racewalk Chairman for Indiana 1964-1966, TAC Racewalk chairman for Wyoming 1983-1990 and USATF Racewalk Chairman for Minnesota 1994. As a chiropractor, he specializes in Quantum Energetics and Applied Kinesiology. He is a member of the Midwest Association of Chiropractic Internists and President of the International Association of New Physiologists.

STRESS

Stress is the key word to most injury. Training or conditioning for competition is a process of adapting the body to stress. Selye described this general adaptation syndrome in the 1960s and it has been well publicized since. However, athletes seldom count all the different types of mental, emotional and physical stresses affecting them in assessing their training and racing capabilities. A divorce, a death of a child, a loss of a job, hot or cold weather are all stresses which add to the adaptation process. A sound training program is adjusted to include these factors.

The most stressful thing that athletes do is race. Once an athlete attains a certain level of expertise and competitive success, he or she looks for more and more chances to race. This excitement leads to over racing.

I have numerous friends who suffer chronic injuries which can be traced back to a specific capital performance, a P.R. or a world's record. Excited by their success, they followed it up with another race and another race close together. Suddenly something "gives out" and they become injured. Sometimes the injury is such that they never recover.

An athlete must keep in mind that injured muscles heal with scar tissue, and that scar tissue tears more easily because it is not as elastic as normal tissue. Muscles also tear a little bit during hard training. Even a minute tear can be extremely painful. It is important to keep such tearing from being replaced with scar tissue.

To maximize healing without scar tissue, athletes want to use natural anti-inflammatories like bromelain. They want to promote good circulation, lymphatic drainage and to take proper rest. They also want to do types of workouts that are not associated with the injury. For instance, rather than doing another speed workout, do a slower session or regular walk.

Speed: At high speed, the body is an intricate balance of mechanical forces. For a very fast walker or for any athlete at maximum velocity, everything needs to be functioning in balance biomechanically. Any small imbalance is magnified by speed. Therefore, speed can create tears in muscles or strains to ligaments and tendons that would not occur at lower velocities.

People often wonder why they cannot build a race car that will go the 500-mile race without breaking down when they have a regular car that goes 100,000 miles. The reason is that the race car is being driven at 200 plus miles per hour. It is going at such a high velocity that the moment a little wear occurs, it flies apart and the engine blows.

Illness: Another common stress that leads to injury is the effects of illness on the body. In our society, increased incidences of flu and colds challenge us frequently. These occurrences do not necessarily make athletes overtly ill. Athletes just recognize that they are not quite up to par, and that their immune systems have been challenged. They will blame how they feel on the "bug going around," think they are fighting it off and continue training as normal. The fact is they may get away with training as long as they do not do a workout that involves speed and overtaxes them.

Injuries often will occur during or immediately following insignificant or small illnesses because athletes do speed workouts or enter races before they have recuperated. I have seen it happen again and again and again. If they had just stayed with less violent work for a few more days, they would have had months of good workouts ahead. Instead they have to deal with rehabilitating their injuries.

We have been telling everybody that racewalking is easier than running, and that racewalking is better for the body. I think racewalking is better for the body because the work is spread more evenly than in running. More muscle groups are used in a more balanced way. However, racewalking is a harder sport to do than running. It is harder to train for. It is harder to do properly and it is harder on the hamstrings and other muscle groups. It takes more concentration and technique awareness.

It is difficult to racewalk at a good speed and carry on a conversation. Runners do this all the time. People can stroll and converse, but they cannot racewalk at an 80 percent effort and converse. Technique and pace suffer.

On the other hand, it is easier to get the heart rate up running. In racewalking, people must be at a certain level of fitness before their heart rates go into their training zones. They simply cannot gain and maintain the velocities necessary for optimal aerobic training until they have mastered the technique and become conditioned. Yet when runners come into racewalking, they have high heart rates because they are so inefficient.

Running is a more natural way of going fast. Strolling is natural, but it is not natural to walk at racewalking speeds. The natural progression is walking to running, not walking to racewalking.

Teaching a person to racewalk is like teaching a horse to be a trotter. Trotters have some of the problems racewalkers have. In galloping, horses have air time similar to our running. In trotting, all four feet are hitting the ground separately. When a vet checks a horse, he will have the horse trot in order to see imbalances. If there is a foot that is compromised, it is readily visible. In similar fashion, it is easier to see imbalances in a racewalker than in a runner.

HAMSTRING INJURIES

Frequently, a hamstring injury is felt below the attachment of the hamstrings to the buttocks, right in or just below the fold of the buttocks. The first sign of injury may be behind the knee, followed by a big pain in the butt.

Based on what I have observed, the hamstrings are amazingly weak compared to other muscles of similar size. Why this is so I am not sure. Take a woman and man to a weight room, lay them on their stomachs and have them do some lifts with their hamstrings. Then turn them over, and have them do lifts with their quads. They will be amazed that their hamstrings are so weak. Comparatively, they might be able to lift 20 to 40 percent more with their quads than they can with their hamstrings.

This seemingly inherent weakness of the hamstrings is often the key to hamstring injuries. It also explains why the body compensates by recruiting the buttocks muscles to help the hamstrings perform. To test the strength of the hamstrings, the practitioner must put his or her arm across the buttocks to prevent any outside assistance from the buttocks muscles.

Racewalking strengthens the hamstrings, but it is necessary to watch for signs of hamstring fatigue. Hamstring fatigue will show up in vague pain and tightness that wander through the hamstrings while an athlete is working out. Sometimes an athlete who has had a hamstring injury will have sensations of tension during a warm-up, a workout, or a cool-down. They will have to stop and stretch their hamstrings frequently. Max Green has told me that he stretches his hamstrings before every interval.

Weight work is probably the best way to counter this fatigue. Stretching, however, is very important. Bohdan Bulakowski has some excellent stretching techniques for hamstrings.

BULAKOWSKI'S HAMSTRING STRETCH

(1) Kneeling, extend one leg out to the side in a 45 degree angle with your toes pointed up. Bend toward your foot and hold for 15 seconds or more. The 45 degree angle is the important component, as this angle makes it possible to stretch the medial, lateral and central bands of the hamstrings. If the leg is extended straight out in front, only one band is stretched. If it is out more than 45 degrees, only two bands are stretched.

Because most athletes do not stretch all three bands of the hamstrings, the band that is not stretched is more apt to pull and tear. By extending your leg in a 45 degree angle from your body and by bending toward your foot, you stretch all three bands equally. I think equal stretching is essential to preventing hamstring injury.

(2) Facing and holding on to a pole, lower your butt to the ground keeping your pelvis close to the support. While extending your free leg straight to the side, let your butt touch the ground. Again, you stretch all the fibers.

HAMSTRINGS AND QUADS

In racewalking, we hear the judges talking about the quads being relaxed. They want the quads to be slack. If they see tension in the quads, they may assume the knee is bent. Of course, weak quads are a better match for weak hamstrings. However, it would be better to go the other way. Let us strengthen the hamstrings to match the quads.

Many racewalkers come from running and their quads are really too strong. There is apt to be considerable imbalance between the quads and hamstrings. These athletes really need to work on their hamstrings by stretching and exercising, stretching and exercising.

THE ANTERIOR TIBIALIS
(Shin Muscle)

Anterior tibialis injuries often involve the spine. The disk between the 5th lumbar and the 1st sacral segment (L5-S1) supplies the nerve root that goes into the anterior compartment. The L5 disk is the narrowest in the body, and its spinal nerve is the biggest. This is simply a fault of human anatomy and creates the problem of the L5-S1 nerve root getting compromised.

Because of the effects of aging, masters athletes have a tendency toward some compromise of the 5th lumbar disk and of the nerve roots supplying the anterior compartment. The anterior compartment contains the shin muscles that lift the foot and toes. When the motor nerves are compromised at the L5, muscle efficiency in the anterior compartment is reduced and toe raising becomes difficult. If the sensory nerves are compromised as well, racewalkers will not have good perception of foot placement. They will think their toes are up when they are not.

A little anatomy may be helpful here. If the spinal nerve is cut in half, the lumen looks like the inside of a walnut. There are three horns — superior, medial and posterior. Two of these horns are motor and one is sensory. If the motor horns are compressed, you get less than optimum motor response and the muscle cannot function. If the sensory horn is compressed, feeling is affected. After a certain point of compromise, there is no remedial treatment possible. That is why they do decompression surgery when a patient has foot drop. There is no alternative.

Put another way the sensory nerves conduct impulses into the central nervous system and provide a direct warning system of overuse and injury. The motor nerves conduct impulses from the central nervous system to activate muscle use. Consequently nerve impairment at L5 makes a walker more prone to shin injury. However, motor nerves can be intact and sensory nerves compromised, and visa versa.

Because the anterior tibialis muscle does not necessarily hurt if it is compromised, a foot-slapper thinks, "Well, nothing hurts me, so it's okay". In fact, his motor nerves are weak. My wife has no pain in her shin muscles, but she has a weak anterior compartment because the L5 nerve supply just is not that good. Consequently she tends to slap her feet and brake her forward progress.

Racewalkers who slap their feet down on the ground need to do exercises and drills that build the strength of these muscles by gradually increasing the stress on them. They are going to have trouble when the rule changes requiring heel first, toes up. Some are not going to be able to do it. They are not going to have enough motor nerve supply and strength in that anterior compartment to hold the toes up.

When the shin muscles begin to tire, an athlete should quit racewalking for that day in order to avoid tearing them. If they continue to hurt, these muscles can be damaged. Putting ice on the anterior compartment when it is sore is suspect. Icing must be done carefully because the nerve is right on the surface. Icing too long can paralyze the nerve, even permanently. When icing gets to the point where the sore area starts to burn, stop.

If you had 100 people in a room, how many do you think would have 100 percent functioning of every muscle and every organ? Probably none. Physical efficiency varies among people. If you have a less than optimum nerve supply combined with a less than optimum nutritional supply combined with an increased level of lactic acid from over use combined with some microtrauma and tearing from speed training, you have a complete formula for injury.

HIATAL HERNIA

The next most common problem that I see among racewalkers, a problem no one is talking about, concerns the diaphragm. According to the statistics I have seen, 60 percent of the American population has hiatal hernias. The most common is a sliding esophageal hiatal hernia. There are other types of herniation in the various slips of the diaphragm, but I think the hiatal hernia is the most frequent culprit.

During competition, I have seen athletes blanch, get white and even vomit. I am convinced that the problem comes from a mechanical dysfunction caused by a hiatal hernia. The diaphragm becomes fatigued and goes into spasm. Either the esophagus is impinged upon by a spasm of the sphincter, or the lung capacity is cut down by intrusion of the abdominal contents into the mediastinum. I have been doing spirometry exams on people before and after hiatal hernia reduction techniques. There has been as much as 25 percent to 50 percent of a liter of air increase after manipulation depending on whether the stomach is above or below the diaphragm.

In simple terms, a hiatal hernia takes up lung space. The stomach sits in the middle of the diaphragm and the lungs cannot fill up.

Before I do a reduction, patients have a spirometry where they blow into a container to measure the volume of air exhaled. Next, I reduce the hernia by doing a soft tissue manipulation that pulls the hernia down and the stomach back into its proper place. When they blow into the measuring container after the reduction, they discover that they can inhale and exhale considerably more air, and of course, air is what walkers go on.

A contributing factor in a hiatal hernia is a compromise of articulation of the diaphragm's attachment to T12. The T12 is where the last rib is fastened and where the lumbar spine begins. The lumbar vertebrae are very unstable because they do not have any ribs to hold them together. Consequently the T12 is often displaced.

Sometimes the twisting and torquing of the body in racewalking aggravates T12 displacement. Sometimes T12 malalignment can be reversed by nutrition and sometimes by an adjustment. Sometimes it cannot be permanently reversed and requires attention on a regular basis. In my experience, hiatal hernia surgery repair does not work very well.

At times hiatal hernias can be reversed if a person avoids having a paunch. A paunchy abdomen can push the stomach through the diaphragm. However, there are slim people who have hiatal hernias so there are no rules. Interestingly enough, if a man has had a paunch all his life, the paunch will not be as much of a problem as it is if he has been slim and acquires a paunch.

George Sheehan, the running cardiologist and philosopher, had two things relevant to say about hiatal hernias. Almost everyone has one and a paunch affects the heart. I think that a paunch affects the heart because it pushes the stomach up into the diaphragm and crowds the heart just as it crowds the lungs.

LOWER BACK

Low back difficulties are common because they arise from an inherent weakness of being biped. Humans have long spines and have arms and legs of varying lengths. This basic skeletal assembly creates leverage problems. For example, if a woman bends over to pick up a 20-pound object and keeps her legs straight, the 20-pound object lifts like 120 pounds because of leverage. The object's weight effectively multiplies five times. Modifying leverage is the principle behind bending the knees to pick up things. Yet, day in and day out, most people reach down, grab whatever they want and create stress in their lower backs that may affect their racewalking.

Another contributing factor to low back problems in racewalking is that humans are right-side or left-side dominant. We have a one-side dominance that is almost to the point of causing a crippling disability on the non-dominant side.

During the growing years, the skeletal muscles of the dominant side pull hard enough to actually make the ribs minutely longer, the head slightly distorted, one eye higher than the other, one shoulder higher and one hip higher. One side of the body may actually have a dystrophy with the muscles of one side greater than the other. Where these disparities are universal, they are not universally equal. They vary from person to person.

The body will make all kinds of adaptations to imbalances, but once it runs out of options, usually between the ages of 30 and 50, symptoms start to surface. The imbalances that have been there all along become accentuated and symptomatic, and injuries will then occur on the weak or non-dominant side just as a chain breaks at its weakest link.

The twisting and torquing movement in racewalking targets the lower back. Older athletes with pronounced disparities in their back and abdominal muscles may develop symptomatic low back problems as they increase speed. They may not have problems racewalking slowly, but when they increase speed, they increase stress on their lower backs and increase the risk of injury.

Whenever athletes superimpose activities that stress their physical imbalances, the potential of injury exits. Once the injury occurs, complete healing may not take place.

Another contributing factor to lower back problems in racewalking is that some people have some degree of wedging in the L5 disk. This means that the L5-S1 vertebrae are not perfectly level. The wedging causes an opening on one side of the disk space allowing the disk to protrude.

The disk is like a shock absorber with a gelatinous center, the nucleus pulposus. If you took the shock absorber in your car and cut the housing out on one side, that shock absorber would start buckling out through the housing. That is the mechanism almost everyone is carrying around in a lesser or greater degree at the L5-S1 level.

When an injury occurs to the disks or to the soft tissues, inflammation starts. The inflammation impinges on the nerve roots as well as on the nerves which supply the muscles above the spine and causes pain. It is not the pressure of bone on the nerves that causes pain as is often thought. When the disks and soft tissue between the vertebrae get out of their space through the wedging, their swelling and inflammation affect the nerve roots and cause the pain.

Because the muscles of the dominant side have created musculoskeletal imbalance, I feel it is better to treat an athlete with a recurrent lower back problem from a muscular imbalance perspective rather than from an osseous perspective. If a practitioner moves the bones, the muscles will just pull the bones back. Bones do not move muscles. Muscles move bones. So treatment and adjustments that reorganize the body's muscle imbalances are more appropriate.

Athletes with lower back problems can do a lot to help themselves. Very careful stretching and exercise is important. All stretching and strengthening should be done on both sides equally and should involve the opposing muscles groups equally.

Bulakowski has some interesting ideas on combining flexions with extensions. He says if you do sit-ups, you should also do back extensions. When you do biceps, you do triceps; when you do the quads, you do the hamstrings. This coupling provides balance to stretching and strengthening.

Athletes can also help themselves by observing their every day activities. Most of us tend to do things the same way so we end up using one side a lot. If an athlete is right-handed, he or she should emphasize dexterity with the left hand. If an athlete is left- handed, he or she should concentrate on using the right hand. If a track workout is scheduled, a racewalker should go one direction half the time and the reverse direction the other half. It is also best to use the 4th and 5th lanes where the turns are not so severe. When I am on an indoor track, I use the 6th lane to remove some of the stress on the inner leg.

The general objective for injury prevention in racewalking is to reduce stress by equalizing imbalances in all activities.

MASTERS WOMEN

BEV LA VECK

RUTH EBERLE

SALLY RICHARDS

PAT NESLEY
NANCY WHITNEY

ELTON RICHARDSON

MARIE HENRY

Bev La Veck

Sally Richards

BEV LA VECK (W55)

Do not race distances you have not trained to do.

Grinding out miles all the time is not the best way to increase performance.

- **I Ultra Distance & Overtraining**
  - **Cross Training, Water Aerobics, Light Weights**
- **II Injuries & Training After Injuries**
  - **Fartleks, 2-Mile Intervals, VO_2 Max Workout**
- **III Training for the Big Race**
  - **Tapering**
- **IV 10Km Training Schedule**

Bev LaVeck is racewalking's national representative to the USATF Master Track and Field Committee. A holder of 40 or so records and an ultra distance walker at heart, Bev holds unofficial track world records in the 100 miles (21:42) and the 100km (11:56). Less well known is Bev's ongoing work validating masters racewalking records and updating racewalking's Age Graded Tables. (See Section V, FACTS ABOUT MASTERS RACE-WALKING.) Masters are indebted to this very special lady and to the statistics she keeps!

ULTRA DISTANCE & OVERTRAINING

The races that I feel the best about are not necessarily those in which I set records. The races I look back on the most fondly and with the most pride are those in which I became closely and forever attached to the other competitors. The 100km and 100-miler were like that as well as shorter races with forgettable times but great colleagues.

I learned a hard lesson in the 100km. I entered the race with the intent of going for a 50km record and dropping out. When I finished 50km, I had missed the record by about one minute. In an effort to make something out of a disappointing situation, I decided to stay in the race and go for the 100km record.

I finished the race and got the record, but I felt horrible afterwards, much worse than after the 100-miler. I still needed help walking two hours later. It was a frightening experience and I suspect my ankles have never been the same since. The message was clear: You do not race distances you have not trained to do!

After the 100-miler, for which I had prepared, I got another insight. Thinking about all the training time involved, I decided that anybody who walks 100 miles has got too much time on her hands and really needs a job. So, I got a part-time job and began walking shorter distances.

I have noticed other changes in my attitude toward training and competing over the years. Now, I think it is more important to assess what is going on in my life before embarking on really ambitious goals. When I was younger and racing the ultras, I was a real mile junky. I kept doing high mileage all the time. I was always ready to race, but never raced really well because I was trying to be in condition for every imaginable distance.

The people I know who have been in racewalking for a long time seem to take a longer view of things. They are more patient and less hard on themselves. They keep their training in balance and consider how best to preserve their bodies and to enrich their lives. Satisfied with what works for them, they have more common sense and self-awareness.

CROSS TRAINING

As a consequence of routinely walking 55 to 62 miles a week. it was getting to be a chore to get out of bed in the morning. I was stiff and sore. I was not injured in the usual sense, but I felt I had to find something else to do besides racewalking. I enrolled in a water aerobics class and in a light weight lifting program. The water aerobics class met three times a week for one hour. Afterwards, I lifted weights for 20 to 30 minutes.

WATER AEROBICS

In this particular water aerobics class, half the people paddle a little and talk about their bridge hands and the restaurants they like. The others do not want to do any exercise beyond a 45-second interval. The class is not very intense. But even at this level, working with water resistance can really develop strength and it is fun. There is lots of pulling the water towards you or pushing it away, and pulling the water up or pushing the water down. In deep water, we hold closed, empty Clorox bottles in each hand as floats. We run in place, do pendulum swings, peddle and kick. It really is more a low impact strength building class than an aerobic conditioning class.

LIGHT WEIGHTS

When I decided to lift weights, I went to an instructor for advice as I did not want to get hurt. Independently, I had tried working with weights a couple of times before, had gone at it too hard and ended up injured. I told the instructor that I wanted to strengthen my quadriceps. I also told her I wanted to strengthen my stomach, lower back, shoulders and chest as I am sure that getting older effects my strength. She gave me this program:

Quads: Leg extensions. Using 10 pound weights, work up to 3 sets of 10 repetitions. I now use 30 pound weights, and do 2 sets of 15 repetitions. If at any time my knee hurts, I stop immediately. The next time I do the leg extensions, I will go back to using a lighter weight.

Shins: Toe lift. I use a piece of equipment called "Hammer Strength." It appears to be especially designed for racewalkers. It strengthens the top of the ankle and shin muscles, and stretches the anterior tibialis when I relax.

Shoulders: Lateral pull-downs. Using 30-pound weights, work up to 3 sets of 10 repetitions of (a) behind the head, and (b) in front to chest. **Front pull-downs**, I have switched to a pull between mid-chest and my lap. This also works stomach muscles.

Pushdowns. Using 20-pound weights, do 3 sets of 10 reps. I now do 1 set of 15 reps using 30-pound weights; then I do 3 sets of 5 reps at 40 pounds.

Lower back: Hyperextensions. Do 3 sets of 10 reps. No weights.

Stomach crunches with variations.

Arms: Biceps curls. Using 8-pound weights, do 3 sets of 10 reps. I now use 10-pound weights.

Triceps extensions. Using 8-pound weights, do 3 sets of 10 reps. Again, I now use 10-pound weights.

INJURIES

The problem I continue to wrestle with is accommodating injuries that have not been caused by racewalking. I am just getting over a gluteal muscle injury I sustained two and one-half months ago chasing a mailman. The injury has interfered with my forward stride. Even if I deliberately try to make my naturally short stride shorter, it is not enough to avoid pain.

With the big summer competitions on the horizon, I have to fight not overdoing. I am forcing myself to pay attention to how I feel every day. Also, I am not making a commitment to do any race until I feel that I am walking and training comfortably. At this point, I still hurt. I no longer hurt so much that I cannot racewalk, but I usually do not stop hurting until I am really warmed up or about 5 miles into my workout. This delay leaves me a very brief window of opportunity for picking up the pace.

I have kept up my water aerobics and weight lifting while I have been injured. Before my gluteal muscle pull, I had noticed that these activities were helping my racewalking times. I had started having mile times and 3000 meter times that were faster than anything I had done in the last two years.

I think it was a combination of reducing my racewalking and of building muscle strength that caused my better times. It is hard to say which made the most difference. I feel that going out and grinding out miles all the time is not the best way to increase performance. It keeps you fit, but it also keeps your body tired.

TRAINING AFTER AN INJURY

At the present time, I am walking a rather pedestrian 12:00 to 13:00 per mile pace for 4 to 8 miles three times a week. When the pain completely goes away, I will start working on pace with interval training. I will keep the water aerobics going, but probably cut back on lifting weights.

Fartlek Intervals: First, I will start doing fartleks, anything from 50 meters to 800 meters, alternating brisk and slow for an equal time. I will never go as fast as I can, but simply pick up the pace so that I am aware that I am working. My main purpose will be to get the feel of changing pace and to get the blood circulating. I will do this workout just about every time I go out, 3 to 4 times a week for 20 to 30 minutes in the middle of a one hour walk.

Long Two-Mile Interval: If the fartlek interval workouts feel pretty good, I will add some variety. One workout I like involves taking my best 5km time for the year and breaking it down to a mile pace. For me this is a 29:30 5km or a 9:30 per mile pace. I add approximately 20 seconds to bring my pace to 9:50 or so and then sandwich 2 miles at this 9:50 pace between slower walking. For example, I will warm up for 2 miles, do the next 2 miles at a 9:50 pace, and finish with a slower 2 miles. Even if I am going to walk 10 to 12 miles, I will throw in 2 miles at that pace, never any faster. Like the fartlek workouts, I might do this two-mile interval workout four days in a row.

VO_2 Max Workout: There is another workout that Gwen Robertson suggested to me that I tried and like very much. This is a track workout for VO_2 max. It is a variable pace workout where you alternate 400 meters at your 5km pace with 400 meters at your marathon pace. The marathon pace is about 15 seconds per lap slower than your 5km pace. You do two or three sets of six with a 4 to 5 minute rest interval.

If I do this workout, I will warm up thoroughly. Then I will alternate 2:18 and 2:35 laps, three times each for 1 1/2 miles. After resting, I will do six more laps. At no point do I go all out. Gwen said never to do this workout during the week you are going to race and do it a maximum of every two weeks, preceded and followed by easy days. Gwen is very alert to people who overtrain. It is really good to have support for not going out and knocking yourself out every day.

An easy day would be 4 to 6 miles at a 12:00 per mile pace. The week I do the variable 400 meter lap workout, I might do a couple of easy days and one long walk with a 2-mile faster paced interval. I might not do too much more than that.

At times, I will pick up my pace and go all out at the end of a track workout. I would rather do fast stuff at the end than early in a workout.

TRAINING FOR THE BIG RACE

Bev, W57, added another Single Age Best to her multiple successes at the World Veterans Games in Miyazaki, Japan, October 1993, with a 10km time of 58:37.

Let me tell you why I think I had a good race in Miyazaki. I usually tell people that they should get some miles in before they do speed. However, after walking 12:00 to 13:00 per mile pace for a few weeks, I was really having trouble walking faster than a 12:00 pace. It was getting hard on my morale. So I decided to do something to get my feet moving.

I started working on speed around the first of June as I decided to enter the weekly 1-mile walks at the local All Comers meets. With this plan in mind, I had to start doing a few quarter mile intervals. I started at about a 9:30 pace. It nearly killed me, and I am sure I could not have walked any farther than a mile at that pace. However, between the 1st of June and about the middle of July, the 9:30 mile went down to 9:20, 9:13, 9:09 and pretty soon it was down in the 8:40's. It was amazing.

I also had decided that I was going to cut my miles back to 30 miles per week for a while. I tried various combinations. I was running on gravel roads and dirt roads at our cabin in the heat and altitude. When I was in Seattle, I would go out for 4 or 5 miles. My longest workout was around 8 miles. The shortest was an interval workout when I would do 8 quarters alternating a quarter at race pace with a slow quarter at a 2:30 or 3:00 minute pace. I did this once a week with a 1-mile warm-up and 1-mile cool-down.

About the middle of July I realized that my feet were moving, but I did not have any endurance. I had not done long miles for nearly two years and had not raced a 10km for over a year. I really was mileage poor and I knew if I was going to walk a good 10km in Miyazaki, I had to add some miles.

As an overall goal, I decided to train for a local Labor Day marathon which was to occur about six weeks before Miyazaki. I began doing 13 miles every 6 to 10 days which worked out to be 6 half marathons prior to Labor Day. I tried to keep my pace 1:30 to 2:00 minutes slower than my 10km pace the year before. During that workout, I put in 2 to 3 miles at a pace that was about 15 seconds slower than my 5km pace. So I did 2 to 3 miles at 9:30 and the rest at 10:50 to 11:50 as the temperature was hot.

I had one or two rest days a week. I always took a day off and perhaps went swimming after my long workouts. The importance of rest days is generally accepted.

TAPERING

The week before I raced the 10km in Miyazaki, I tapered in a way that was completely contrary to my nature. I just took a flying leap of faith and followed a training schedule that Gwen Robertson pulled out of one of Jack Daniel's articles. In this tapering schedule, you do not do any junk miles.

As you read the schedule, keep in mind when I do quarters, I do not stand around for a few minutes between them, but usually racewalk slowly. I started tapering six days prior to the race.

Day 6 - 5 fast quarters
Day 5 - 4 fast quarters
Day 4 - 3 fast quarters
Day 3 - 2 fast quarters
Day 2 - 1 fast quarter
Day 1 - none

This was all I did and it was really hard sticking to it, especially when you are around others who invite you to accompany them for "a couple of miles." I marked off a quarter-mile course in front of the hotel and every night about 6:00 p.m. I went out to do my taper. I think I missed one day in travel, but otherwise kept exactly to this schedule.

There were other ways I focused for success. When I got to Miyazaki, I did not do any of the social activities. I did not go to the Opening Ceremony as I did not want to stand around or sit around in the hot sun; nor did I want to tire myself by parading around the stadium. I also did not sign up for any of the dinners with the people of Miyazaki. I find that I put out a lot of energy on social things just being around people. I did not even go over to the track and watch other competitions. I generally was not very friendly.

I also got a rail pass for the five days before the 10km. Every morning I went over to the train station. I did not care where I went, I simply wanted to return by 9:30 at night. If I got tired sitting, I would get off in the little towns and walk around for a mile or so to loosen up and then get back on the next train. I stayed out of the heat, I stayed away from people and I stayed off my feet before the race.

The morning of the race, I could see that it was getting hot. I was one of the few who took a jug of water with them. Instead of drinking one-half hour or hour before the race, I drank a good slug of water, about three cups, just before we had to line up for the start so that I would not have to urinate before the race. I had a hat on and a scarf around my neck to protect me from the sun. Besides all this preparation, I had not raced in so long I was really looking forward to it.

1994 Update: I used the same training schedule I used for Miyazaki for the U.S. Masters Championships in Eugene, Oregon. This included training for and competing in a hot-weather 20km in late July. I made a Single Age Best (W58) in the 10km racewalk in cool weather. My time was 57:56.

10KM TRAINING SCHEDULE

Bev adapted the following workouts from the notes of her Coach, Gwen Robertson. Bev stresses the importance of combining quality and rest, and not doing the same old grind day in and day out.

A. **STEADY WALK** - (70-85% of weekly mileage)
   1. 9 or more miles @ 1:30 to 2:00 per mile slower than 10km race pace.
   2. Less than 9 miles on recovery (easy) days.

B. **LACTATE THRESHOLD** - (6-16% of weekly mileage)
   1. Tempo workout for 20-25 minutes, 15 seconds per mile slower than 10km race pace.
   2. 5-mile walks, 10 seconds per mile slower than 10km race pace.
   3. Tempo Plus, 8 minutes (4 seconds slower than 10km pace) 6 minutes (1:30 slower than 10km pace.)
   4. 1 mile x 4-5, 15 seconds per mile slower than 10km pace with a 1-minute rest between each mile.

C. **INTERVALS (VO2 MAX)** - (8-10% of weekly mileage)

1. 2-5 minutes at 5km pace with equal recovery time for 4-5 minute interval; slightly less recovery for 2-3 minute interval.
2. Variable Pace. Do 400's alternating between your 5km pace and your marathon pace (23-28 seconds slower)
   Do 2 or 3 sets of 6 (2 sets roughly equals 3 miles).
   Do not walk faster than 5km pace. Do not do this more than every 2 weeks. Precede and follow with easy or rest days.
   Do not race the week you do this workout.

D. **REPETITIONS, Economy** - (5% of weekly mileage)

1. 200-400 meters, 30 seconds faster than 5km pace. 1 minute of recovery for every minute of fast walking.

E. **TAPERING BEFORE A MAJOR COMPETITION**

1. Reduce training by 60% during last 2 weeks. Six days before competition, warm up for 1 mile, do 5 x 400 at 5km race pace with walk recovery until you are ready for the next interval. Cool down 1 mile. Subsequent days reduce intervals by one. Day before rest. (See page 129)

EXAMPLE TRAINING WEEK FOR 10KM

- 1 day, a long 9 miles, 1:30-2:00 per mile slower than 10km pace
- 2 days, easy 4-5 miles. Possibly add fartleks on one of these days
- 1 tempo day (2 miles, 15 seconds per mile slower than 10km pace. Do during a 6-mile walk.)
- 1 interval day of 8 x 400 with a 2-mile warm-up, 40 meters easy walk between intervals and 1-mile cool-down.
  (Equals about 6.5 miles)
- 2 days rest and other activity.

L to R: Ria Marsh,
Ruth Eberle,
Lauchlan Ales

Marie & Dan Henry

L to R: Bev La Veck, Elton Richardson, Nancy Whitney

RUTH EBERLE (W60)

I am not losing my speed by reducing my number of workouts, in fact, I may even be gaining speed because I am rested when I do race.

I am always stretching.

I Quality Not Quantity
II Competition
Stretching & Eating Before a Race

Ruth Eberle holds the 1-mile American Age-Group Record (W60) at 8:47; the 10km at 59:43; and 5km at 28:34. At the Indoor Nationals in 1994, she walked a 3km in 17:17. 1995: At the World Veterans Games in Buffalo, she won the silver medal in the 5km at 30:04.67; and the silver medal in the 10km at 63:49. She is coached by her daughter, Gwen Robertson.

QUALITY NOT QUANTITY

Gwen started me racewalking. I had just turned 53, and she told me that I should stop jogging because it probably was not good for me. I am a teacher and cannot set a weekly schedule like some people can. My hours vary and I can get in only three to four workouts a week.

Gwen has taught me that overtraining is bad. I think I overtrained at the beginning, and I realize now that I was really hurting myself. Now, I do no more than two hard workouts in seven days. I will go for seven miles, or maybe I will do a VO_2 max type workout consisting of 4 repetitions of 1000 meters at race pace. It could be eight times 400 meters or it could be six times 200 meters.

Before the racing season starts, I develop a strong base just by walking a lot. At this time, I will only do one day of intervals. Around March when I know I will be doing a lot of competing in May, June and July, I begin working out at least four days a week. I will do two hard days, one of intervals and maybe a longer distance closer to race pace, but not race pace, just closer to it. I always hold back a little. Easy days I will walk at about a 12 minute pace for 3 or 4 miles, or I may jog for 3 or 4 miles.

When I was 53 to 55 and had just started to racewalk, I found it hard to resist the compulsion to train much more. It was okay at first because I was strong, but now that I am getting into my 60s, I need to have rest days to get my strength back between workouts. I feel better, and it is showing up in my race times. I am not losing speed by reducing my number of workouts; in fact, I may even be gaining speed because I am rested when I do race.

If you are not happy racing because it hurts you, you are not going to want to compete. I try not to overtrain because that will hurt me. Then when I go to races, I feel rested and ready. I feel that with the little extra I put forth, I am capable of winning.

COMPETITION

It was not competition that got me into racewalking. I wanted an activity that I could do by myself whenever time permitted so I could maintain my good health. I do not have problems with my bones as some women do. I do not take food or mineral supplements, but I do take Estrogen as my doctor prescribes.

I love racewalking because it gets me outside. It gives me an activity that is not dependent on somebody else and one that I can fit into my varied schedule. Often if you are dependent on others, you end up not working out as much as you want. But as important as convenience and fitness are, racewalking gives me time to think, relax and plan.

Most women are a little fearful of competition. I think one reason is that most do not know how to pace. I am a pretty good pacer. Learning to pace is part of my training. I very seldom wear a watch on my wrist and can closely estimate what speed I am going.

When I am pushing out at my full power during a race, I know my speed is about a 9:30 to 10:00 per mile pace. If you study my lap times, they are almost identical. Gwen has trained me to do this. She has me do my quarter intervals at a pace 5 seconds slower than my race time. As I train, this pace becomes natural to me. In competition, I hope to go faster because I am pumped up, but I know confidently what I am capable of doing.

I have a competitive spirit. I do not want anybody ahead of me whom I know I can beat. If someone is ahead of me, I will not try to catch them in the first lap, but they are in my sights. I know if I keep on pace, I will be where I am supposed to be at race end.

I would like to emphasize that I am careful not to start out too fast in a race. Some people dart out in front. I will not do that. I start out and finish on pace. If I intend to do the loop of a 10km in 15:00 and I come around at 15:10, I know I have to go just a slight bit faster in the remaining loops.

As I usually race against younger age groups, I am normally third or fourth at the beginning. I try to keep as close to the leaders as I can. It is a psychological thing. If you do not want somebody to pass you, it is better not to be in the lead, especially if you are not the fastest in the field. Watching people pass can cause you to lose heart. Start out and keep your own rhythm and pace. In this way, you catch the competition that has gone out too fast, and they have to deal with the psychological problem of being passed.

When you are young, you can count on a sprint at the end of a race. Older women cannot. As a person gets older, the best way to improve finish times is to keep making the pace a bit faster during workouts. This way, you know that you can go a little faster if you have to because you have done it in your practices.

By late spring and early summer, I usually am working out pretty hard because there are a lot of races in St. Louis before the Masters Outdoor Nationals in July or August. I use these local races as part of my training. The races will be hard days and I will just have one other hard day that week. The week or so before the Nationals, I taper off. I racewalk for fun the last four or five days. By then, my training has been completed, and my focus is on resting for competition.

If you are not ready a week or two before the race, you are not going to be ready. No last minute efforts will matter. It has been proven that on race day you get the benefits from the training you did two weeks beforehand.

STRETCHING & EATING BEFORE A RACE

When I first started racewalking, I did not stretch. Now, I stretch whenever I think about it. I am always stretching this way or that. I do the usual overall body stretches. When I am teaching, I stand a lot and need to stretch all the time. I will stretch in the evening for a while. This way you keep your body limber all the time.

When I am warming up before a race, I always walk one mile or one and one-half miles. I will stretch a lot and then maybe do a little speed work. Not a whole lot. I do not want to wear myself out.

I eat a very normal all-round diet. I eat what comes naturally in variety. I do not eat before a race. I might have a piece of toast three hours before if it is a long race. This is personal. Some people need to eat, but for sure, do not eat much before a race.

SALLY RICHARDS (W40)

The masters community is really a role model for what could be in racewalking. The good will, camaraderie and mutual support regardless of age or race times is sport at its best.

I Athletic Background
II Racewalking, Benefits of Technique
III Competition
IV Training, 2-week schedules, Fartleks, Speed
V Masters Racewalking

Sally, a resident of Colorado, is a relative new comer to racewalking. Competing in both the open and masters division, Sally picked up gold medals at the Masters Outdoor Nationals in Spokane in 1992, 5km 25:32; in Provo in 1993, 5km 24:48, 10km 50:49; and in Eugene in 1994, 5km 24:24 and 10km 50:38. In 1993, she set masters records at 15km in 1:20:06, at 10km in 49:19 and at 5km in 24:13. She was selected as the Outstanding Masters Woman Racewalker in 1993. In 1994 at the WAVA Road Race in Canada, she set a New American 20km Record of 1:52:07. In 1995, at the WAVA T&F Championships in Buffalo, Sally took the silver medal in the 10km with a time of 53:59.

ATHLETIC BACKGROUND

I have always been athletically oriented. I grew up in an athletic family, and living in Colorado, took up skiing early. I raced in Vail where they had an excellent junior program. I made the U.S. developmental team and like many, had Olympic aspirations. Unfortunately, when I was 15, I had a ski accident. My leg was very badly broken and never healed properly. Though I continued to race, it was a real hindrance.

Graduating from high school, I decided to attend the University of Grenoble in France to study French and to ski in the FIS University Circuit.

The French ski team took me under their wing and I travelled with them as there was no U.S. team participating in this circuit. The European ski teams had a reciprocal arrangement that lead to a wonderful camaraderie. For example, when the French team went to Austria to compete, our expenses were paid by the Austrians; and when they came to France to compete, their expenses were paid by the French.

While living in France, I married a French medical student. When he finished getting his degrees, we came back to this country so he could practice medicine here. We had two small babies, 13 months apart. However, I felt frustrated as I had not reached my athletic potential in skiing because of the broken leg.

I took up running and soon was running marathons. I really enjoyed running and did fairly well from 1978 to 1992. By 1992, I had four children. I was thinking about settling down and giving up competition, but, again, I could not shake off my lifelong desire to prove myself athletically.

RACEWALKING

I am a Christian and definitely believe in God's will and messages. I was walking in the woods one day, and out of the blue came this big word, RACEWALKING. I said, "What? You have to be kidding!" The thought of racewalking kept reoccurring and I became very curious about it. However, I was too hesitant to even try it in my neighborhood. So I went down to a local race where I thought no one would know me and jumped into a 5km with the racewalkers. Within 20 yards, I had the newest respect for the sport. I could not believe it. I considered myself a fit person and I was suffering. I realized there was a lot more to the sport than meets the eye.

I had a lot of accumulated athletic experience when I started to racewalk. My skiing background helped because I had developed good body awareness. I had spent many years focusing on muscular development and on the different parts of my body working together. I also had spent many years competing and being out-of-breath so that feeling was not foreign to me.

At first, I did not know what I was doing. I had this mental image of racewalkers in an Alka Seltzer commercial that I saw in the 1960s. I had not seen the sport done live and knew nothing about the rules. I was coming in at ground zero. What I recognized was the sport's tremendous potential for fitness and competition. I thought racewalking was fabulous and was hooked.

BENEFITS OF TECHNIQUE

I am basically self-coached, but not by design. I did seek out instruction, but did not find very much where I lived in Colorado. I got hold of some videos and tried to learn on my own. In the process, I discovered that the racewalking technique was very compatible with my physical attributes.

All through the years, my broken leg had remained weaker than the other. I had tried to strengthen it, but never really succeeded. In fact, my running aggravated the imbalance as running relies almost entirely on the legs. In racewalking, you use your whole body. You also have to move symmetrically in order to perform. I found I could use my upper body strength to compensate for lower body weakness. This worked well as my torso was very strong. Most importantly, I found that the technique was helping me strengthen my weak leg.

There are two levels of racewalking — fitness and competitive. You can pick the technique up quite quickly for fitness benefits, but getting into the higher levels of competition is definitely a different matter. It takes a long time to perfect the movements. Competitive racewalking is an intellectual challenge as well as a physical challenge, and the challenge is ongoing. You cannot put yourself on autopilot. My dilemma in 1992 was that I did not have a clue as to what to work on as I trained.

I was getting to a level where I needed some really good coaching beyond recreational coaching. The first real coaching I received was at the 1992 Masters Outdoor Championships in Spokane. Martin Rudow was a judge and I asked him to give me a few pointers. He said, "It's amazing you have done as well as you have. Your technique is terrible." He noted that I had a lot of athleticism which was carrying me. The good news was that he felt if I improved my technique, I could definitely improve my times.

In the spring of 1993, almost six months after Spokane, I met Dan Pierce. He was trying to start a club and do some coaching. He had group workouts which included intervals. I was familiar with training concepts from running, and it helped having more structure to my training.

Because I had made the Women's National Team in 1993, I was able to go down to the Training Center in Colorado for their camp. I learned that I do not have a particularly long stride, but I do have a really fast turnover rate. People get the idea you should have long legs to do well in racewalking. You do not. Debbie Van Orden, Michelle Rohl, the Mexican women and the Chinese women are perfect examples of short women with fast turnovers. The turnover rate is the key.

I also learned I do not have a high $V0_2$ max, but I do have a high capacity to maintain my aerobic threshold for a long period of time. I do not possess a lot of upper body strength, but I do have quite a strong torso. I have very strong abdominal muscles and a strong back. These strengths have been a real boon in racewalking because they have an important stabilizing effect.

I can speak much more on my weaknesses. Like all of us, I have problems getting loose in the shoulders and in the hips. I was very stiff when I first started racewalking. After four childbirths, I was starting to develop arthritis in my hips. My doctor told me to forget running because after every workout, I could not walk the rest of the day. I would agonize every time I had to bend over to pick up something the kids left on the floor. Racewalking totally got rid of my hip pain.

Racewalking demands flexibility. The pelvic rotation required the use of ligaments and muscles I did not even know I had. As my muscles began adapting and my circulation improved, my stiffness and pain got better. On occasions I still have some lower back pain. Then I know that I have to do lower abdominal exercises. After doing them for a week or two, the pain subsides.

The racewalking arm movements help tight, sore shoulder and neck muscles. And I should not overlook posture. To be fast and efficient, you have to have good posture. I had horrendous posture. Racewalking has helped mine. You need to think of yourself as longer and taller than you are.

COMPETITION

The first year of competition, I surprised myself. Every race I entered my times improved. Initially I was thinking, "Wouldn't it be incredible to win a race." Soon I discovered I could. Someone told me I ought to try out for the Olympic Trials. This was in 1992. I had only been racing a few months and answered, "Give me a break. The Olympic Trials!" Then I thought, "Hmmmmm." Ever since I could remember, I had the dream of being in the Olympics. To even think of being in the Trials seemed like such an honor, such a dream.

Almost by chance, I signed up for the National Invitational in Washington D.C. at the end of March. The qualifying time for the Olympic Trials was 50 minutes. I finished in 50:36. I did not make the Trials, but I was pretty close.

That summer, someone asked me if I was going to the National Masters Outdoor Championships in Spokane in August. I did not know there was a masters circuit and asked, "What's that?" I found out and mustered up the courage to go. I was first in my age group (W35) in the 5km, and second overall with a time of 25:32.4. This was very exciting to me and really convinced me to start training seriously.

In addition, I found the enjoyment and dedication racewalkers find in their sport and in each other very refreshing. Some sports are very elitist and cutthroat. Athletes are competitive not just during, but after competition as well. They essentially feel they are enemies. To me that is not the spirit that promotes a sport.

In this country, athletes racewalk because of a genuine interest in and love of the sport. They are definitely not looking for prestige and financial awards. I find this observation amplified in masters racewalking. Masters racewalk both to compete and to enjoy each other socially. Everyone feels a sense of community — that we are in it together.

TRAINING

My training is always unique. I am the only person on the National Team with four children, not to mention being 42-years-old. I have to plan carefully and it is a real challenge. As I do not have many hours for training, my training has to be very specific. My natural tendency is toward long distance. I can go out on the roads for hours where I live because it is so beautiful. It is a pure joy. What I have to do is discipline myself to do speed work on the track.

I plan a year in advance. The last two years, I have been competing in both the open circuit and the masters circuit. For example, the 1995 competition schedule started with the US Outdoor Championships in mid-June, followed by the Masters Outdoor Championships the first weekend in July, the World Veterans Games mid July, and the Olympic Festival the last weekend in July. The IAAF World Cup of Racewalking was in April with the 10km trials for the World Cup Team in January.

In October of 1994, I began training for the World Racewalking Cup 10km Trials in Florida. I was working with an excellent running coach in Texas who gave me a very balanced workout schedule. Initially, I did more cross training. My workouts four months from the target race were:

TRAINING SCHEDULE, Four Months to Target Race

Monday	A run.
Tuesday	15 x 400 meters at a pace faster than my 5km race pace with a 90 second rest.
Wednesday	Cross country skiing.
Thursday	A moderate paced two hour walk.
Friday	Running or walking 7-8 miles at about 75%.
Saturday	2 x 5km.
Sunday	Fartleks.
	Generally, the schedule consisted of 3 hard walks, 2 quality runs, and 2 recovery days skiing or biking.

FARTLEK WORKOUT

I particularly like the fartlek workout my coach gave me. It is very balanced. Warm up 15 minutes or so. Do 4 or 5 repeats of 4 or 5 minutes at a 10km pace with a 3-minute recovery between intervals. Then bring it down to 4 or 5 repeats of 3 minutes at a 5km pace with a 90 second rest. These fartleks are followed by a 3-mile tempo walk at 80 percent.

It is a long workout. It may sound horrible, but it is great! It is very nicely balanced and is probably one of the best I have done. You get a good rest between the intervals. You build up to the shorter and faster fartleks, and by the end, you feel good doing the last 3 miles.

I have done better since balancing racewalking with running and skiing. Racewalking is wonderful because you use so many muscles. If I just racewalk, however, my hamstrings get very strong and I lose my quads. The running keeps the quads strong and balanced.

TRAINING SCHEDULE - Two Months to Target Race

In December, eight weeks before the World Cup 10Km Trials, I dropped one run and added another walk. In January, I started doing 5 days of walking, one day of jogging and one day of skiing for total recovery. As I added more walks, I added more shorter, faster stuff. Two weeks before the race, I was doing easy walking with a little speed. The week before the race, I rested.

SPEED WORKOUTS

When I do speed workouts, I have specific time goals for different phases of training. For example: If I am training to do a 10km at 48:40, my speed intervals are related to achieving this time. When I do two speed workouts a week, I will do:

(1) A long workout - 5km on a track at race pace, or
10km at race pace.
(2) 6 - 10 x 1000m at a specific pace.

The only problem I had with the training schedule for the World Cup 10km came from the running. When I got back on the track doing speed work, I really had to concentrate on not lifting. When you are running up hill all the time, you strengthen those muscles that jump you up in the air. I had to pay close attention to maintaining ground contact when I was racewalking at race pace. As the month of the Trials approached, I had gotten back on the ground and felt balanced muscularly.

MASTERS RACEWALKING

Logically, I should not try to do both the open and masters circuits. However, I enjoy masters racewalking so much. To me, it is sport as it should be. I enjoy the support, the encouragement, the whole atmosphere, and do not want to give it up.

The masters have really discovered the legitimacy of the sport. There is a lot of support for masters and it is great to see the numbers out there. We racewalkers need to look at ourselves as being involved in a legitimate sport. It seems as though a lot of racewalkers go around apologizing as though they were second rate. What comes across is that they do not feel racewalking is quite a legitimate sport. As anyone who has ever tried to racewalk knows, that is not the case. If all of us can get out there and positively promote our sport, it is going to help everyone.

One of the things I love about the masters racewalkers is that everyone has incredible stories and have overcome something. As a mother of four and twice divorced, I have empathy for the problems people have. Many of us get very discouraged about our bodies, about life, and about our futures. I have seen racewalking perform miracles for people who thought they never could be athletic, who did not know where to go for weight loss, who had lost their self-esteem. Racewalking is very accessible to everyone. I appreciate and respect the elite aspect of the technique at higher levels of competition, but I also appreciate the accessibility of it for people generally.

If there is one woman who is out there setting a role model in racewalking, then others can say, "Hey, she can racewalk. Maybe she understands. Maybe I can give this sport a try. Cool. Maybe I can get my friends to give racewalking a try. Maybe, they can feel better about themselves, too."

One of the biggest things I would like to emphasize is that I feel very fortunate to be where I am. I think we all need to look at racewalking as a blessing and work together to promote the sport. The masters community is really a role model for what could be in racewalking. The camaraderie, the good will, and the support of the masters for each other regardless of their race times or ages is sport at its best.

PAT NESLEY (W65)
NANCY WHITNEY (W55)

Younger women express a lot of interest in my racewalking and are fascinated that an older woman looks well and walks competitively. - NW

In the process of competing, you prove to yourself that you can get through hard times and reach your goals. - PN

I Why Racewalking?
II Post Season Rest & Early Season Start Up
Lower Back Injury, Camps
III Women and Competition, Competing on the Circuit
IV Training
Heart Rate Monitors, 10Km Workouts, Nutrition, Senior Olympics, Competitive Spirit

Members of the Potomac Valley Walkers in the Washington, D.C. area, Pat and Nancy spent 1994 travelling the national championship circuit winning medals and making friends wherever they raced. In 1995, Pat (W65-69) won a gold medal at the 10km Nationals in Niagara, NY, 67:43; gold medals at the Masters Outdoor Nationals in E. Lansing, MI, 5km 33:20 & 10km 68:39; and a silver and bronze at the World Veterans Games in Buffalo, NY, 5km 32:59.18 and 10km 68:48. Nancy did not race in 1995 in East Lansing or Buffalo due to a persistent lower back problem.

WHY RACEWALKING?

Nancy: I first saw racewalking on television. European racewalkers were being featured, and I thought the sport looked very interesting. However, I did not take time to pursue it then. Some years later, I spotted an advertisement for a racewalking clinic in our Washington newspaper. I went to the clinic and liked the sport immediately. I did not have any trouble with the technique and decided it would be fun to learn how to walk faster and more efficiently.

Pat: I was a field hockey player and a La Crosse player. I got into long distance running in my fifties and ran several marathons until I was injured. Like Nancy, I also saw an advertisement for the Potomac Valley racewalk clinics. I said to myself, "Well, I am not going to sit still. I am going to try this." And I became hooked.

In my mother's generation, women did not do sports as we do. They seemed to get to a certain age and their health would start to deteriorate. They would have problems with gaining weight and with arthritis. It was a vicious circle for them. Observing my mother, I decided that I was not going to be that way. My credo has been, "I want to do the best I can for myself because I am only here once, and the once I am here, let's see what I can do with it."

I also feel that some day I may have an illness or accident and my body is going to say, "You took care of me, now I am going to take care of you."

POST SEASON REST, EARLY SEASON START

Pat: Nancy and I did many races last year. If we were not on a plane going somewhere, we were racing at home. Around Thanksgiving last year, I felt I needed to take some time off. It takes a while to get back into training after deliberately taking a rest, but that is okay. I think after a heavy competitive season, it is good to clear the cob webs away and do something different. Then, when you feel ready to start training again, your motivation is up.

Right now, I am getting back into speed work. It will take a little while. I realize that I am a little older and cannot rush it too much. My times are not what I would like them to be and this is one of the reasons I decided to attend a racewalking camp this year.

Nancy: I have had to take it easy for a while because I am injured. I have a lower back problem, a pinched nerve with sciatica that goes all the way down to my foot. I am fine once I get on the track and get my circulation going, but I have been avoiding speed work.

I went to a chiropractor for treatment a couple of times. As I have to sit a lot at work, he recommended that I get up and move about more. He also recommended massage and the whirlpool. It is just a matter of doing what he says. Also, I am going to start doing abdominal strengthening exercises again.

Last year when Pat and I raced all over, I did abdominal exercises quite regularly. I have not done any this year because I thought they might be bad for my back, but the contrary is true. Coach Bohdan Bulakowski convinced me that I should start them right away again. He feels strongly that they will help me recover as they helped him recover recently.

CAMPS

Nancy: I like to go to camps early in the year. They redirect me toward what I have to do to get ready for the competitive season coming up.

Pat: I think we are always looking to fine tune the things we know. Every coach you meet is going to give you something to think about and try. Some things will work and some may not work for you. It is a continuous learning process. I find camps very stimulating and really enjoy meeting the marvelous people who attend them.

The good coaches are pretty much in agreement about the basics of technique and training. There are some differences, but you expect that. You always pick up information that is new to you.

WOMEN AND COMPETITION

Pat: Women are apt to be more shy about competing than men. However, once women get over feeling unsure of themselves, many become hooked on competition. Frequently all that is needed is encouragement from those who have walked in their steps. I will tell a new person, "Your technique has really improved. Why don't you try a 3km race. Don't worry about your time, just see if you can finish." Women respond to someone showing interest in them.

I did not race when I was learning. I did not have the confidence. I needed to be encouraged to race. About five years ago I realized, "Hey, you have to do this for yourself, so go out and do it." I did and I have been racing ever since.

Nancy: A club can be important in encouraging women to compete. If a club's coaches want women to participate in local races and notice when they are not there, it can make a big difference. Often women just need to stop worrying and to make up their minds to try. When they do enter a race, they usually find it is fun. Pat and I compete for fun as well as for self-improvement.

It is interesting how my racewalking affects the women at work. I have a very demanding job in marketing and really have to squeeze every minute of every hour in a day. The company I work for is very much an image type of company and we have to dress up and look just so. The other women in the company are much younger than I, 30 to 35 max. They express a lot of interest in what I do, and are fascinated that an older woman looks well and walks competitively.

I think it is helpful for younger women to know that as they get older, they do not have to fall apart. They hear my message about staying fit mentally, emotionally and physically. You see, I really believe that all three go together and they know this.

Those of us who racewalk are really ambassadors for our sport. I think it is important to take every opportunity we have to spread the word. If racewalking is not what a particular woman wants, I encourage her to try running or to try the jumps and throws. However, I think women's racewalking is growing in numbers and popularity.

COMPETING ON THE CIRCUIT

Pat: I encourage women who like to compete to take a chance and travel to the regional and national championships. I tell them, "If you are worried about coming in last, that's okay. Almost every new walker feels that way. However, the chances are you will do much better than you think."

Nancy: Pat and I have actually regretted not going to certain races. We have not gone because we thought we were not quite good enough. Then we see the results and say to each other, "We could have gotten gold medals if we had gone!" What matters is who shows up, not necessarily who is the best in the country.

TRAINING

HEART RATE MONITORS

Pat: Nancy and I love to work with a heart rate monitor. Using a monitor is the best way to improve. We each have one and have been training by our heart rates for over two years. Before that, we would try to use the pulse, but by the time you find your pulse, you have already dropped ten beats or so. Pulse taking is not as accurate as a monitor. Our coach, Bob Ryan, no longer uses the formula 220 minus your age. For well-conditioned athletes, he uses 230 or 236 minus your age.

At 67, if I am doing a long, slow Level I workout, I will stay between 120 and 140 beats per minute. If I am doing an intermediate or Level II workout, I try to keep my heart rate between 150-155. Level III, my speed zone, is between 155-160. I have gotten up to 164 beats per minute, but that is max. I do not feel too well at that rate and have to pull back. My race pace is about 92% to 95% of Level III or 150 to 155 beats per minute. I cannot race above my maximum heart rate too long or too often.

I do not wear a heart rate monitor when I race. I want to know my body well enough that I can tell how fast I am going. I do not want superfluous things distracting me. I want to stay focused and to concentrate on such things as what my knees are doing, what my feet and toes are doing, and what my shoulders are doing. I have a tendency to be very tight in my shoulders so I try to focus on relaxing them. I also work on keeping my head up. I go through a little check list. I believe in doing this as I feel it really pays off.

Nancy: At 59, my maximum heart rate works out to be quite a bit higher than Pat's. That is the reason it is important to be tested individually because ranges vary, not just between ages, but between athletes in the same age group. My heart rate for a Level I workout goes up to 155 beats per minute. Level II is 155-162. Level III is 165 to 170. If I get up to 173 beats per minute, I am working hard, but it is okay. If I want to sprint, then I can go to 180, but I cannot sustain that effort. So an efficient, strong race pace for me is around 162 beats per minute. I am working well at that heart rate.

Pat: Nancy and I had blood tests done for lactate acid. We went to West Virginia and worked with Clark Campbell who is a swimming coach and physiologist. He did three separate blood tests on us. One was done after we took an easy walk around the track. The next was done after a moderate effort. The third followed an all out effort. He charted our blood chemistry at these heart rates and worked out a training program for us.

What Campbell found was confirmed by another test we took later. Dave McGovern had us go as fast as we could around a track at race pace for 10 minutes. He told us when to stop, we called out our heart rates and he recorded them. We did this three times in all, each time calling out our heart rates after 10 minutes of racing. My heart rate stayed the same at 157 and Nancy's stayed in the low 160s.

A heart rate monitor is very helpful because it gives you control. For example, some days I cannot push myself up to what my heart rate should be for my scheduled workout. On such occasions I simply say to myself, "I cannot do this today." Everybody who uses a monitor experiences days like this. If the flu is lurking, it shows up during training. Your legs feel too tired. You have the overall feeling, "I just don't want to be here." The heart monitor provides a warning mechanism that objectifies how you feel.

WORKOUTS FOR 10 KILOMETERS

Pat: In training for the big summer 10km races three months away, I am doing one long distance 20km per week to gain confidence that I can finish my races. Twice a week, I do speedwork and get my heart rate up to where it should be for as long as it should be. The other days of the week, I like to do six miles at 70 percent.

There are two speed workouts that I like particularly. One is simply doing 4 x 800 meters. A killer is a ladder workout where we do 100, 200 and 300 meters with short rests between the intervals. We do this once a week with maybe 3 repeats. You can feel the lactic acid building up because your legs start getting very heavy and tired.

Nancy: We often tailor our speed work to a target race. For example, if we are aiming for the 10km Nationals in Niagara Falls, we start our speed training with 1-mile intervals. As we get closer to the race, we begin decreasing the distance of the intervals and increasing the speed. So first, we build a base with slower mile intervals and then we start the shorter, faster intervals.

Besides the speed workouts Pat mentioned, we may do: 10 x 400 or 12 x 400. We may mix this up with 4 x 800, 4 x 400, and 4 x 200 meters. When we mix the shorter and longer intervals, we always try to do about 3 miles of speed work.

Pat: I usually take one day off a week unless I feel that I am coming down with the flu or something. Then I will take two. As I mentioned, I am trying to use some wisdom. I have gone through stress fractures from overdoing and am convinced that if anyone pushes it far enough, something is going to give.

Nancy: About three weeks before the targeted race, we start tapering. The week just before the race is very quiet. We will do 2 x 800 meters maybe on Tuesday and Thursday. Nothing to tire us out, but enough to maintain our high level of racing fitness.

Pat: Because I feel it is so important, I would like to stress the wisdom in not forcing yourself to push on days when you should not. There are days when your body tells you to back off and go easy or rest. On other days you will feel so good, you will say to yourself, "I did speedwork yesterday. Why not do some more today?" It is important to remind yourself, "If I do two hard workouts in a row, I am more apt to pull a muscle and become injured." That is why it is so helpful to get a program that is based on your heart rate, age and gender.

NUTRITION

Pat: I confess that I like something sweet. Some time my blood sugar gets down and I just feel like something sweet. I do not feel there is anything wrong with eating sugar as long as you do not overdo it. I specifically do not use sugar with ice tea now.

I am trying to cut down on fat. I go without butter on my bread. I use Catsup instead of butter on my baked potato which is not bad. I try to eat lots of salads and use very little or no salad dressing. It is surprising how you can adapt. I will have steak every once in a while, and I eat a lot of fish and chicken.

Nancy: I take a lot of vitamins. I take 1000 units of vitamin C every day. In the Washington area we have a wide variety of pollens. When you are outside training hard and breathing heavily, you really get exposed to them and I think vitamin C definitely helps control my allergies. I also take Vitamine E, a multivitamin and hormones.

SENIOR OLYMPICS

Pat: We enjoy going to the National Senior Olympics. I know there has been quite a bit of controversy over the numbers of disqualifications given the last couple of years, but I think there should be better judging at the grass roots level. It is unkind not to disqualify illegal walkers at home. People spend a lot of money for airfare, housing and food. Their hopes are built up by their apparent success, only to be dashed by good judging at the Nationals. Some get so disenchanted that they give up the sport and we do not want that.

I wish the message could get out to the people responsible for putting on the local qualifying Senior Games to have proper judging for the walks. The problem is that some meet directors do not even know the rules of our sport or what judging involves. Consequently, the walkers in their meets have no way of knowing what they need to work on to become legal. Good judging would prompt bent-knee walkers to improve so that they could have a good experience at the Nationals.

Nancy: There are many elderly ladies who just plain walk, and they get disqualified because they do not know what racewalking is. When I qualified at the Maryland Games, several walkers kept saying, "She is running." They had no idea what I was doing. They thought I was cheating and were angry about it.

Pat: Where I live in the District of Columbia, they have two walks. One is a 1-mile fun walk which anyone can enter. The other is a 1500 meter judged walk which is the qualifying race for the National Senior Olympics. If you enter the judged walk, you must know proper racewalking form. If you do not know it, you can expect to be disqualified. The competitive walk is first. If some people are disqualified, they can enter the fun walk afterward. If they really want to learn to racewalk, they are invited to attend the clinics of the Potomac Valley Walkers.

THE COMPETITIVE SPIRIT

Pat: I have always had a competitive spark to do the best I can. I feel when you compete, you want to see what you can do against other people. Therefore, you keep pushing yourself to another level. You are focusing on discovering what you can do. You meet one goal and then you say, "I think I can do better than that." With long distance running, I started doing five miles. Then I thought, "Well, if I can do five miles, I can do seven." Pretty soon I was up to 10 and then 16 miles. Somewhere along the line, the idea of doing a marathon took shape.

If you keep setting goals for yourself, it may take a while to reach them. When you do reach them, you know that you are one of a very small percentage of people in this country, or even in the world, who has done what you have done at your age. It gives you a feeling that if something difficult comes up in your life, you will be able to handle it.

Nancy: In the process of competing, you prove to yourself that you can get through hard times and reach your goals. You prove to yourself that you can succeed.....

Pat: ..... and not give up. Sometimes, you will get in a race and worry, "I don't think I can do it." Then you say to yourself, "Come on. You have trained. You have gotten this far. Just try to get up to that lamp post or to the other side of the track." Pretty soon you find yourself crossing the finish line and you say to yourself, "I didn't think I could do it, but I did it!" The next time you face a situation that you feel you cannot do, you will know you can!

ELTON RICHARDSON W55

I plan to racewalk the rest of my life. I will never turn back. It is a very happy addiction.

Elton Richardson (W55) of New York City holds 23 national championship titles and 21 American Records. In 1994, she won eight national championship titles (3km, 5km, 10km, 10km, 15km, 20km, 40km, 1-hour) and set nine American Records 3km 16:24, 5km 27:53, 27:30, 10km 57:58, 57:26, 57:24, 56:36, 30km 3:12, 40km 4:28, 1-hour 10,253m; and 2 world records 3km 17:28, 20km 2:00. In 1995, Elton won the gold at the Masters National Championships in East Lansing (W55) 5km 29:15, 10km 58:11; and was a triple gold medallist at the World Veterans Games in Buffalo, 5km 28:30, 10km 58:31 and W55 Team.

NEAR INVALID TO WORLD CHAMPION

I started running at age 48. I was recovering from osteomalacia, adult Rickets, and had been sitting around being careful not to overexert myself in order not to make my condition worse. Then I heard a running club director on the radio talking about 65- and 70-year-olds running marathons and how much fun they had training in Central Park every Sunday. I decided that I, too, could become active.

The running did not bother my osteomalacia which surprised me, and I ran three marathons in the next two years. In fact, it actually strengthened my muscles and bones, and I found I had been careful for nothing.

During this time, I started watching the walkers in the club and concluded that racewalking was not only a beautiful sport, but it was much less stressful on the body. The fact that the racewalkers were not pounding the pavement attracted me, and I thought racewalking could be just as much fun as running.

I was coached by Bruce MacDonald for three years. I have also had sessions with Ron Laird, Don DeNoon, Dave Romansky, Gary Westerfield and Martin Rudow. Otherwise, I workout pretty much by myself.

TRAINING

I train and race all year long, but am starting to ease up in November and December. I am learning the importance of resting. Normally, I train five to six days a week. It depends on my target race and how I feel. I will have one very hard speed workout and one lighter speed workout a week. These workouts are hard because they are all out.

HARD SPEED WORKOUT: Total mileage is 3 to 3 3/4.

1 2 x 1km, 4 x 440, 4 x 330, 4 x 220.
2. 6-8 x 440, 6 x 330, 4 x 220, and 8 x 100.

LIGHT SPEED WORKOUT:

1. The same distances as a hard workout, but fewer and slower intervals.
2. 3 miles with 10 or 12 accelerations. For example, if I am going an 11:00 per mile pace, I will accelerate to a 10:00 pace for about 100 to 150 meters. I will recover for the same distance and accelerate again.
3. Speed Plays. Run a few yards and walk a few yards never stopping. Do this for 1/2 mile, recover, and do another 1/2 mile.

A WEEK WORKOUT SCHEDULE

Sun. Long distance. The amount is related to the distance of my next race. As I am presently training for the 40Km Nationals, I did 20 miles this Sunday.

Mon. 5-6 easy miles. If my body tells me it is tired, I will just have

	active rest in which I will do some weights or go to the gym, but no walking.
Tues.	Hard speed workout.
Wed.	6 miles, moderate speed. I may go to the gym and do stretches, crunches and weights.
Thurs.	Light speed workout.
Fri.	6 moderate miles, go to the gym and do stretches, crunches and weights.
Sat.	Rest or light gym and stretches

I added the total hours and discovered that I am doing between three and four hours of training about two times a week. For example, I try to workout in the early morning because my body and the air are fresher. So I am out before six o'clock and will walk for 1 hour and 15 minutes to 1 hour and 45 minutes. At noon I will do 30 minutes of weights. After work, I will do 1 hour and 30 minutes of stretching and crunches when I go to the gym. All that adds up.

I may train six days a week before events like the Masters Outdoor Nationals or the World Veterans Games. My training is as described above though I cut the long walk to 14 miles when my target race is 10km. As the race gets closer, I tend to favor 6-8 x 440, 6 x 330, 4 x 220, and 8 x 100. One or two weeks prior to the race, I will do a test race.

The week of a major race, I taper. I might do a light speed workout midweek. For example I might do 1km's at a 5:45 pace rather than a 5:30 pace, especially if I have done a test race the previous weekend. The two days prior to the race, I just go out on the track and walk around a couple of times at a slow, easy pace to loosen up.

MARATHONS

I really like to race long distance. I especially like the 40km, and I know how to train for it. Since I have done marathons, this race is not hard for me. The discipline is there.

I train six months for a marathon and increase my mileage gradually. My long walks start at 12 miles. I will stay at 12 miles a few weeks and then add 2 miles. Right now my longest training distance is 20 miles in preparation for the 40km. The 40km is 24.8 miles, just a little shorter than a marathon.

At Don DeNoon's suggestion, I did something different the month before the 40km last year. He suggested that I do two faster 10-mile workouts instead of one long 20-miler. He said that I was training the slow twitch muscles doing the 20-milers and that when it came to the race, my muscles would behave accordingly. So, to get my fast twitch muscles going, I did fast 10-milers twice a week. This year I am sticking to the 20-miler once a week. I feel more comfortable putting in the long miles.

NUTRITION

I am not a person prone to injury. I attribute this both to my training and my nutritional orientation. I am a vegetarian, but I eat fish and eggs and occasionally dairy. If I get a craving for cheese, I go get some, eat it and forget it. Same with yogurt. However, dairy is not a regular part of my diet.

I also believe in supplementation because I believe that we are putting a lot of stress on our bodies, especially those of us who are very serious competitors. I believe that nutritional supplementation will counter the affects of the stress.

I am a great believer in 'good ol' vitamin C, not only for the immune system, but for building the cells that tear down when we train. Yesterday after my 20-miler, I took 5,000 mg or two teaspoons of powdered, buffered vitamin C with bioflavonoids. Besides the vitamin C, I take vitamin B_{15} (also known as DMG or dimethylglycine) before every race which you can get in any health food store. The DMG prevents cramping. I also take electrolytes which replace the minerals lost in perspiration. The drink I use is called Electrolytes.

I have been taking DMG and Electrolytes ever since I became an athlete. In addition, if the race is 10km or longer, I take Coenzyme Q10 and L-carnitine for the heart as my heart rate really goes up. I eat very little fruit because of the sugar or fructose. I have a sweet tooth and a half, so fruit is my "brownie." I do not use table sugar. When I bake, I sweeten with bananas or apples.

In Eugene at the 1994 Nationals, they were very considerate of vegetarians. I stayed in the dorm and there was so much I could eat in the cafeteria. Usually, I take my food with me as I am concerned about eating the right things.

MENTAL AND SPIRITUAL ADDICTION

I plan to racewalk the rest of my life. I will never turn back. It is a very happy addiction.

As a youngster, I was the world's biggest klutz. People laughed at me and my three feet. I hated P.E. because I was so clumsy. Being an athlete is all new for me. When I started running at age 48, I would not compete for almost two years. They kept urging me to "Get in," and I finally did. I started winning 3rd place and then one day, I got first. I kept calling my mother after every race to tell her how I finished.

I come from a very spiritual family (the eighth of thirteen children) so I have a very deep spiritual foundation that sustains me. My mental preparation includes a lot of spiritual affirmation. When I do my long workouts, they are less boring because I sing songs that I learned as a kid in Sunday School, and I repeat my favorite scriptures.

The sport is spiritually uplifting to me. It has given me discipline. I have a brighter outlook on life. I look at people differently. I am more tolerant. When I am training, I see beautiful images. I see the little faces of my nephews and it makes me smile. It makes a workout a pleasure and not a chore.

I am very happy to be able to look forward to racewalking each day. It is a way of reaffirming my health and my strength. I think of 1984 and how I could barely walk with the osteomalacia and of the surgery in 1985. I am a new person for being an athlete. I feel beautiful inside.

Pat Nesley

Nancy Whitney

Elton Richardson

MARIE HENRY

Quite contrary to popular thought, I do not think older women have any conflict between being competitive and being feminine. I think they are much more secure in a lot of things than younger women.

I Competition
II Racing Success
III Overcoming Fear of Being Last
IV Profile of An Athlete
V Women and Racewalking - From the Male Perspective By Don Henry

As of May 25, 1995, Marie Henry, a resident of New Jersey, holds the USATF W60 Age-Group 10km Track Record at 1:09.00, the (W60) 40km road record at 5:07:09 and the 50km record at 7:27:49. At the height of her competitive career, she made many single age best performances, many of which still stand. Marie's unique point of view and humor gives her a special place in women's masters racewalking. Marie was interviewed in 1990 when USA Track and Field was called The Athletics Congress (TAC).

COMPETITION

I do not enjoy competition whatsoever. I know there are many masters women who do enjoy competition, but I am not one of them. I have never enjoyed it. However, when I get in a race, I do my very, very best. It does not matter whether the race is national or local. Whenever I think I can pass somebody, I will give it my best shot.

I started competing because at some point I knew if I did not compete, I would not train. Competition motivates me to keep training. It gives me discipline. I have spoken with other women about this. Some look at me with "Oh, go away!" written all over their faces. Others understand. But I know what is inside of me.

Many times when I am training, women will stop me and say, "I want to walk like that." I might be walking in the park or in the supermarket. I racewalk everywhere. At first I used to spend 30 minutes or so trying to show them how to racewalk. But I learned a valuable lesson about not wasting time. Now, I find out how interested they are by asking, "Why do you want to walk like I do? What is it you want to do? What is your purpose?"

If they say they want to go fast and compete, then I answer, "Are you willing to put in long hours of training? Are you prepared to dedicate a lot of time to it? Are you prepared for the discipline that is involved?" Then, I ask, "Are you willing to have a brain drain? Are you willing to put aside things that you know are very, very important, and put them on the back burner?" You see, I feel these are the requirements for being a good competitive racewalker.

It comes down to what you want to accomplish. If you do not have a goal, racewalking is not the kind of activity you just start. I mean if you really want to feel fit, okay. But do not even talk about racewalking competitively unless you want to find out what you can do and because it makes you feel good doing it.

RACING SUCCESS

I think when you get into a race, if you are not prepared mentally and physically before the race, you will not be able to put it together on the start line. Again, I can only talk for myself. I try to concentrate on getting myself in a fairly good position at the beginning of a race and then on walking the very best I can.

While competing, I check myself from the very bottom of my feet to the top of my head to make sure that all my body parts are working to the best of their ability. As I had prior training as a dancer, I am aware of muscle power. This awareness is a definite advantage in racewalking. I concentrate on using my power maximally.

I have been competing for 9 years. During this time, I made Age Best Performances at 58 and 59 and was still setting records at 65. At that time, I had to take care of my father and had to let competition go for a year. When my father died and I returned to racewalking, there was a definite change in my attitude.

I was just as willing and eager to racewalk, but not as keen about competition. Perhaps I had reached a point where I had nothing more to prove. I had attained all my goals though I did not realize it consciously. Now, I occasionally enter a race, but speed is not my goal as much as enjoying myself.

I love to racewalk. I love the sense of movement, the sense of freedom and rhythm and the joy of getting outside and walking. I also become very creative when I am racewalking along the roads. I was and still consider myself to be an excellent stylist. To me, style plus speed is what racewalking is all about. It is what separates us from the fitness walkers. I think it is a beautiful sport, and I just love doing it.

OVERCOMING FEAR OF BEING LAST

I do not think you can really motivate anyone to go into competition. A person has to have some inner interest or desire to race. I think you either are competitive or you are not.

Quite contrary to popular thought, I do not think older women have any conflict between being competitive and being feminine. I think they are more secure in many things than younger women. If they do have a problem, I think it is embarrassment and fear that they will look slow and funny competing. Women are apt to see themselves as wives, mothers, grandmothers, housekeepers, everything and anything, but not as athletes.

You have to be confident in yourself to get out there when others are watching you. With me there was never any choice. I saw racewalkers and I wanted to do what they were doing. However, I had to gain confidence, too.

How you think you look racewalking influences the way you feel about yourself. When I first started, my daughter said, "Oh, Mom, racewalking is so swishy." If you think racewalking looks swishy, you will feel swishy. If you do not think that way, and I certainly do not, this attitude shows. I think racewalking is a beautiful, rhythmic sport and I feel good doing it.

Oh, sure, I got a few cat calls when I first started out. Someone would go by and call out, "Hey, go for it mama." But it was more rough encouragement than derisive. Their calls reflected my attitude toward racewalking and the confidence I have in my ability. I know I look good and it shows.

When I first raced, I would defer to runners if it was a mixed race. I would move over. I would put my arms down so as not to poke them in the ribs. Then all of a sudden I said to myself, "Hey, why am I doing this? I have as much right to be in this race as they. I am an athlete. I deserve and have earned a right to be here."

Also at first, I found it embarrassing to have the ambulance and police following me because I was last in a road race. Then came the day when I waved them on and that was a big step forward. I felt I knew what I was doing and that I would make it to the finish line.

Confidence takes time in coming. The important thing is to tell a new walker, "Just get out there and do it." What an older woman gets from racewalking evolves. At the point when she feels the joy of racewalking, she may chose to become competitive. Personally, I think the older woman athlete is coming into her own.

PROFILE OF A TRUE ATHLETE
by Marie Henry

My husband, Don, is much more of an athlete than I am. He cares. He cares about competing and always does his very best because he loves sports. But this is just one part of it. For the last few years, he has not been able to compete because of injuries. The closest he can get to being active is doing things for TAC (USATF) and for racewalking. On the weekends, he goes to track meets to officiate and does his best to make sure that the athletes are treated well. It is this love of sports and the willingness to be part of sports, if not as a competitor as a supporter, that singles him out as a true athlete.

WOMEN AND RACEWALKING FROM THE MALE PERSPECTIVE

By DON HENRY

In 1990 Don Henry was appointed to keep the official, certified TAC (USATF) masters racewalking records for men and women. His efforts (along with those of Bev LaVeck) were behind the initial package of Masters Age-Group Records submitted to the TAC Annual Convention in Seattle. Prior to this appointment (1986-1989), he kept the Best Age Performances for masters women.

What do you think attracts older women to competitive racewalking?

Fitness. They start walking seriously for fitness and are attracted to racewalking as an outlet for their training. Becoming competitive is a consequence of wanting to be fit. A man goes into competition because he likes to compete.

Have you noticed that women over 55 are more reluctant to get into competition than younger women?

Older women are apt to worry about being last, about holding people up. Also, they may be reluctant to compete because televised sports always show professional or elite athletes performing. The 55-, 60- or 70-year-old woman says to herself, "Who am I? I am just starting and I don't want to look foolish."

This is especially so if a woman has never competed when she was young. She gets butterflies that the guys have long since gotten over. Even going out to train, she wants to hide in a pack.

What would you say to a 60-year-old woman who expresses interest in competing, but has doubts?

I would take her to a race and show her that there are people her age and older racewalking, and that they do not look foolish. I would introduce her to these people and let them talk to her. She will find that they are having a good time.

One reason I have supported masters racewalking over the years comes from every day observation. When Marie and I go to the supermarket and see older people barely able to hang on to their carts, I know that with a little exercise they could become more fit. And I am not just talking about physical fitness. I am also talking about mental fitness. Competitive racewalking requires mental fitness, alertness and discipline. I think it is a shame to see people deteriorate when they have choices.

MASTERS MEN

STAN CHRAMINSKI

JIM CARMINES

DON DENOON
RAY FUNKHOUSER

ENRIQUE
CAMARENA

ED KOUSKY

MAX GREEN

BOB MIMM
DON JOHNSON

GIULIO DE PETRA

STAN CHRAMINSKI M45

Your body only has so much in reserve. Once you have used up your reserves, you will break down physically and mentally and it will take a long time to heal and regroup. It is better to back off earlier, at the beginning of the downside, so you can come back the next season strong.

I Training
- **Mileage**
- **Lydiard's Periodic Training - Periods I-IV**
- **More Is Not Necessarily Better**
- **Consistency**

II Scheduling
- **Cross Training, Other Interests**

III Race Preparation - Tapering, Warm-up, Judging

Stan was born in Germany. His parents were in German labor camps during World War II and stayed to help with resettlements before coming to the U.S. in 1952. He grew up in New Jersey and is a longtime resident of Seattle, Washington. He has completed a total of 38 marathons and 50km's, and only dropped out of one in 1986. His favorite marathon is the Honolulu where he has placed third overall twice and second overall once with times between 4:12 - 4:15. "Always one young guy around to beat me."

In 1994 he was ranked 11th in the U.S. in the 50km and has set many long distance track records. In addition, in 1991, M40, he placed 1st at the 15Km National Championship in Oregon. In 1992, M40, he was 2nd in the 5km and 20km at the National Masters Championships in Spokane. In 1993 and 1994, M45, he was 1st in the 20km in Provo and Eugene. Since 1985, Stan has coached masters runners at the YMCA. He hopes to retire in another decade from his job as an Insurance Trainer to a life of painting, racewalking and writing.

TRAINING

MILEAGE

I enjoy training and competing. My kids are grown and I only work a 40-hour week with a short commute so I have as much time as I really want to devote to racewalking. My training mileage has been dropping the past few years as it takes longer to recover from hard workouts and racing. I have been doing 2300 to 2700 miles a year, about 80 percent racewalking. I have found this mileage takes about as much time as it used to take running over 3000 miles. My top week ever was 92 miles last year when I was training for the 50km. I find now that the long walks needed to train for long distance leave me too tired to do much else that day so it is harder and harder to get motivated to do them.

Training mileage depends on how much your body can tolerate and what distance you plan to race. If you are training for a 50km, you want to walk at least as long as you will be racing for several workouts. For me, this means five-hour walks of 25 to 29 miles. If you are training for 20km, you want to do some overdistance walks. For example, if you are planning your finish time at about two hours, walk at least two and one-half hours regularly in training. You want to be able to deal with the fatigue and concentration needed in longer races. The speed of the workout is not as important as being on your feet for the amount of time of the race and getting used to eating and drinking while walking.

LYDIARD'S PERIODIC TRAINING

I believe in Arthur Lydiard's periodic training. You should divide your year into seasons with a period for rest, a base period to build strength, a period to work on hill repeats and longer speed sessions and finally a peak period of speed work and racing. This works well for masters when the key racing season is the late summer masters championships. You can use the winter to build your base and the spring for hills and speed.

Period I - Active Rest: After a racing season, you will be stale physically and mentally. Take a few really easy weeks at about half your average mileage to get a rest while maintaining some basic fitness. Do other fitness activities such as swimming, biking or hiking instead of racewalking. Then, once you feel revived, begin your base building period.

Period II - Base Building: During the base building period, speed is unimportant. Walk how you feel. The key is to build strength by increasing your mileage. I have found a three week cycle works best, both in this phase and throughout the year.

Weeks can be broken down into a cycle of long-medium-short mileage. Start with 40-30-20 miles a week, 40 the first week, 30 the second week and 20 the third week. Gradually build your mileage by adding 5 miles a week to each cycle, 45-35-25. A good base phase to aim for is 60-50-40, then repeat. By following a long-medium-short cycle, you can plan to do other things on your short weeks. If there are any races during the base building phase, work them in so they are in your short week. This way, you will be rested and can get decent results even though you are not doing speed work. The good races come later. Continue this base phase for several months.

Period III - Hills & Strengthening Drills: This is a transition period to speed training. If you live in a hilly area, choose a course where the hills are spaced fairly evenly. Push each hill hard, but maintain proper racewalking form because you do not want any bad habits to develop. Slow down on the downhills to save your knees.

An alternative is to find one decent hill about 200 to 300 yards long and to do repeats up and down. Begin with about 4 to 5 repeats and over the course of a month or so, work your way up to 10 to 12 repeats.

Hill work is optimally effective if done twice a week. If you race during this time, you should expect to be slow due to your hill workouts. After 5 to 6 weeks of hills, come down to the flat land.

The final transition phase to speed work and racing starts with a series of drills to increase strength and pace. Find a dirt or grass stretch about 100 meters in length. You do repeats using about 50 to 60 meters in these workouts. The following three drills should be done twice a week in sets. Gradually increase the number of sets or increase the distance. Start with three complete sets and work your way up to five or six sets.

Strides. Concentrate on stride length through hip rotation. It is almost straight legged running so do not worry about staying legally on the ground. Get the stride as long as possible while also keeping up a good cadence.

Sprints. Shorten your racewalk stride and go for fast turnover. Train your muscles to fire up quickly. Racewalking is more about turnover than anything else so concentrate on this drill. You may need to start with a few yards of running sprints to get the turnover and then change to racewalking.

Form. After the above two drills in which you are not concerned about staying legal, put stride and turnover together maintaining excellent, legal form. In other words, walk quickly while staying legal. The goal is for your judged racewalking to improve.

A month's worth of these three drills twice a week and you will be ready to do good speed training and racing.

Period IV - Speed Training & Racing. Speed training is best on a track. Initially emphasize longer distances such as one mile. I have found that a 5km is a good workout on the track. This makes use of your stride and lets you develop and maintain smoothness. The proper 5km workout pace is about a 10km race pace.

The last phase of this training period is short intervals. These intervals are intense and are used for sharpening before important races. Do repeats of 400 to 1000 meters at a 5km race pace or better. The goal is to feel smooth at your fast pace.

This overall training program should leave you with the strength to hold a good pace through a 10km or 20km. This phase will not last long because at some point after a series of hard races, you will top out and reach your peak for the year. More hard training will only make it worse.

You can extend the racing phasc if you rest more and do less workout mileage. Easing the work load will keep some freshness in the legs. The races will maintain your fitness. Eventually, however, you will have to back off, rest and begin the cycle over again with long, slow distance.

During the hill and speed work phases, do one longer walk on the weekend, especially if you are training for 20km or over. However, you will want to keep to the weekly cycles of long-medium-short overall mileage. If you keep the same level week to week, you will probably always feel tired.

MORE IS NOT NECESSARILY BETTER

Do not get into the trap of thinking you will keep improving if you just keep training hard and racing often. Frequently a new runner bursts on to the national scene, cleans up in a year of road races, and then is not heard from again for several years. Most often he or she has violated these rules. Your body only has so much in reserve. Once you have used your reserves up, you will break down physically and mentally and it will take a long time to heal and regroup. It is better to back off earlier at the beginning of the downside so you can come back the next season strong.

In 1993, I started training for a 50km in December, and never took much of a break until after the Masters Nationals in the late summer of 1994. By fall, I was exhausted. It took over six months to recover physically to where I could race well again, and even longer to recover mentally to where I wanted to race. That is why I am skipping the Nationals and World Games in 1995. I am healthy, but just do not feel like the heavy training necessary to guarantee fast times.

CONSISTENCY

Consistency in training is an important element, too. If you back off before getting a major injury, even if you cut back to just a minimal level, you can maintain good fitness. I have found you can improve in racewalking by just being in the sport consistently over the years.

Train hard when you feel like it; for example, 60 miles a week. Train minimally when you do not; for example, 25 to 30 miles a week. My friend and fellow racewalker, Bob Novak, just set another 10km P.R. this month doing low mileage and minimal speedwork because he has stayed healthy and consistent.

I have not trained below 30 miles a week in several years. (A few of these weeks, I mainly used a NordicTrack and Stairmaster to recover from minor injuries.) Like Bob, I can race successfully up to about 10km relying on my long-term training consistency.

Even during my six months of downtime when I had no desire to train hard or race, I kept on doing 30 to 40 miles a week of slow walking and jogging. You can maintain a strong base and even get stronger if you do not lose weeks or months of training because of injury, or get so stale that you do not workout at all. Then, when you feel like getting back into racing a

20km or 50km, you start from a good level of fitness and your body only needs to make minor adjustments to the higher work load. It is better to view the sport long-term than to concentrate on one shining season and be forced to drop out all together.

SCHEDULING

I believe in a hard-easy schedule, not only day to day but week to week and even year to year. This ties into the three-week cycle recommended earlier.

Alternate your days and weeks between hard and easy, and race at the end of your easier weeks. We all will have different definitions of a hard or easy day. During 50km training, a 10-miler may be an easy day. At another time, the easy day may be a 3-miler slow and a hard day may be a 10-miler. Generally, race days, speedwork days and double digit days are hard at any pace.

You can sometimes do several hard days in a row. For example, you may do a longer walk on Sunday after a short race on Saturday because it is the only way to fit in a long walk. But, I have found that you usually pay for it with some nagging injury or excess fatigue. It is better to skip the longer walk on a race weekend and do it midweek or the next weekend. The art of training is figuring out your own limits and staying within them.

As a masters competitor, I have found two hard days a week manageable and three if I am feeling especially good. Sometimes, I will not do any hard workouts in a week if I do not feel like it. Usually, however, after three to four easy days, your body cries for a little speed and you want to do a harder workout. As I get older, I find the recovery times are getting longer. Listen to your body and get the rest you need.

CROSS TRAINING

Most any form of exercise is helpful for racewalking as long as you do 60 to 75 percent of your mileage walking with good form. I have heard of young walkers who run most of their training mileage and just do their walking as speedwork. This may be all right for those who have no trouble maintaining good technique during competition, but inadvisable for those who have technique problems. I have found too much running tightens up my knees and causes technique problems.

As you get older, cross training becomes more and more important in maintaining overall muscle mass and fitness. I have a full complement of machines at home and run twice a week. I have found the NordicTrack the best for a quick overall workout on rainy days and a rower useful in building upper body strength.

Most exercise machines are boring, even with a TV right there to watch. It helps to put in a one-minute sprint every five minutes to maintain concentration. During one injury, I could not walk, but I could do the NordicTrack. I worked up to an hour on this machine with frequent sprints. When I started racing a 5km again, I found I had not lost any fitness and could use the one-minute spurts to pull away from a close competitor. Sit-ups and stretching should complete your cross training workout.

OTHER INTERESTS

I have learned the importance of having other interests to take your mind off your training and racing. It is good to be dedicated, but too much dedication usually leads to problems. If you are fitting your training around other interests, you will have to train efficiently and not waste time. Make your easy days easy. Save energy for work, family, poetry, or for whatever you love to do.

I have had an art business going the past few years in addition to my day job. I schedule myself to paint on my light workout evenings when I have the time and energy. On hard days, I get serious, do the workout well, and quit before I am completely shot. I always try to leave a little water in the well.

RACE PREPARATION

I have found prerace preparation to be very important. I have a three day schedule that I like.

3-DAY TAPER

Three days before the target race, do 2 x 1 mile at about a 10km race pace. Emphasize smoothness versus going all out.

Two days before the race, do some short strides of 50 to 100 yards within a 3-mile walk. Focus on turnover for one stride, hip extension for another, and then stride length. These strides are like the drills mentioned earlier.

The day before the race, just walk 2 to 3 miles with 3 to 4 repeats of 400 meters at about a 10km race pace. You want to feel smooth and easy walking a good pace, but do not go all out.

Toward the end of the racing season, this tapering program will be too strenuous and tire you. Just do the strides the day before to get loose and leave it at that.

WARM-UP ON RACE DAY

I have found it useful to do a 1- to 2-mile loosening walk several hours before the race. I will include up to one minute of strides at race pace. This prerace walk works especially well when warm-up time is limited before the race. If I have to get up earlier than 6 a.m. to warm up for a race, I will do some loosening drills the evening before. Some of the benefits seem to carry over.

Just before the race, I have found it useful to do strides, but for only 30 to 40 yards at a time. Then, I will do about 400 meters at near race pace about 10 minutes before the start. This short fast interval is especially good for a short race such as a 5km where you can not waste time getting up to speed. It gets rid of shin spasm and other muscle stiffness which may plague the early stages of the race.

The last thing to remember is to double or triple tie your shoes. You have probably experienced flying shoe laces at some time, so do all you can beforehand to avoid this distraction.

JUDGING

I recommend always concentrating on form over speed. I often meet newer walkers who refuse to give up speed to learn proper form. Because of their impatience, they never race successfully. Speed comes after form. If you cannot get your knees straight, then racewalking is not for you.

I feel judging should be tough to keep the sport legitimate. If your biomechanics are not right, find another sport. I enjoy basketball, but at my size I do not have any illusions about being competitive. It is no use complaining that everyone is too tall or the basket is too high. It is the same with racewalking. Some have the body for it and some do not. You are better off looking for some other sport where there is a better match of your skills and the sport's requirements so you can compete successfully.

As racewalking is an artificially limited form of running, I sometimes question the need for the sport. However, I am grateful that it does exist. It fits in with my own attributes and I can enjoy training and competing. It has the advantage of needing more varied skills than many other sports. Speed, endurance, coordination, mental toughness, rhythm and dedication are all needed to succeed as a racewalker. Maybe it is this need for so many abilities that limits our numbers more than any other factor.

Stan Chraminski

Jim Carmines

JIM CARMINES (M50)

The hardest element of the technique for me to learn was the hip rotation. It took me nine months before I could get the hang of it and was able to rotate at will.

From Don DeNoon I have learned that there is no age limit to what you can do. You can excel within the potential of who you are yourself.

I Learning the Technique
II Training
Tapering, Heart Rate Monitors, Camps
III Competition
IV Masters Racewalking

Jim Carmines started racewalking in 1990 and started to compete seriously in 1991. He burst on the national scene quickly, settling with the silver medal only when Don DeNoon was racing. In 1995, he won the gold medal in East Lansing, MI, in the 5km with a time of 23:43.66. At the WAVA Games in Buffalo, he placed 2nd in the 5km, 24:01.07, and 4th in the 20km, 1:52:24.

LEARNING THE RACEWALKING TECHNIQUE

Before I started racewalking, I had always enjoyed taking long recreational walks. When I developed plantar fascitis from jogging, I went to walking and found that it did not bother my feet. I began pushing myself to try to walk as fast as I had been jogging which was about an 8:00 per mile pace. I had gotten down to a 12:00 pace when I heard about racewalking. I met some racewalkers and started getting some of the literature.

The hardest element of the technique for me to learn was the hip rotation. It took me nine months before I could get the hang of it and was able to rotate at will. My first priority was getting the needed flexibility in my hips and lower back, and I concentrated on stretching these areas. You have to be able to move your hips before you can control their use with your mind.

On the weekends when I was doing my long, slow distance workouts, I would practice hip rotation and the other elements of the technique for 100-meter stretches. I would shift focus from my arm swing, to foot placement, to keeping my leg straight, to hip rotation, to posture and so forth. I might concentrate on speed for 100 meters and then rest for 100 meters. I kept going from one focus to another as long as I could, but always back to my hips.

At first my hips would not cooperate. I would stop for a moment, think about how I wanted them to go and start up again. At the end of nine months, they began to feel right. I remember that day well. I was doing a 100-meter focus on my hips and knew I had the rotation right. It felt so good. I immediately did four laps concentrating on my hips and discovered at the end that I had taken a full minute off my 1-mile time. Afterward, I kept repeating to myself, "I've finally got it!" I went home sore that day, but very satisfied. I had learned how to control my hips and also how to get more pushing power with my feet.

When I am asked to describe the hip rotation, I use a very simple analogy. The more technical people call the hip movement, a "drop" where you move the hips forward and drop them in a circular motion. To me it feels more like a washing machine agitator going front-back. I do not feel a drop in my hip. I just feel front-back, front-back.

Evaluating the technique, I think that your legs give you 60 to 70 percent of your effort in a race and you pick up another 10 to 15 percent from good arm movement. Many people are not getting the pace they want because they only use their legs, or just 60 to 70 percent of their resources. If they would use their hips, push with their toes and use their arms correctly, it would all add up to better times.

TRAINING

I have a training program that rotates on a two-week cycle. Many people do the same thing each Monday, Tuesday, etc. In my schedule, only Saturdays, Sundays and Mondays are the same.

Saturdays	Long distance of 14-18 miles.
Sundays	Recovery days of 5-7 miles at a much slower pace.
Mondays	Off. Weight lifting.
	The remaining days have a variety of intermediate and speed workouts.

On my days off, I lift weights. About 15 years ago, I benched 225 pounds, currently I bench 135 pounds ten times. As my upper body is still strong, my weight lifting is much heavier than I would recommend for racewalking. I encourage people to use 5 to 7 pound weights to develop their arms, and 30 to 40 pounds for benching. I do Nautilus and free weights for my legs.

Speed: I try to do at least one speed workout each week all year long. As I get closer to the shorter races of 3km and 5km, I may do two or even three speed workouts a week for three weeks. You do not lose endurance just before a race, and you can gain a lot of speed by doing multiple speed workouts.

As I always train for a 20km, my speed work is for a 20km. I usually do 1/2-mile intervals because the course that I use is marked for 1/2 mile rather than for 1km. I will do ten 1/2 miles which is similar to doing eight 1-kilometers. I like longer intervals because doing short 100m and 200m repeats just gets you off the start line. If you do ten 1/4 miles, you have only gone 2 1/2 miles. When I do ten 1/2 miles, I have gone five miles and am approaching half of a 20km race. If I do a 5km race, I look at the race as only six intervals.

When I do my speed workouts, I do them on the flat. Sometimes I will do them on a track, but most of the time I do them on a measured course along a river front near where I work.

Everyone has their own training techniques. Some people find ladder workouts very effective. I know when Don DeNoon does his interval workouts on a track, he starts a ladder workout at 100 meters and goes up and down. It is a question of individuality. I like the 1/2 miles because I feel they give me the endurance to do what I need to do for a 20km.

Long Slow Distance: I also support the theory that doing some long, slow distance on an incline offers excellent leg strengthening. Maintaining proper form going up hill is good for me. However, downhill can be hard on the legs, especially if it is steep.

I have a 1/2-mile course around my housing development and the downhill part is very steep. I will go down with a bent knee to protect myself. Fortunately, the downhill is only 30 seconds while the uphill takes four to four and one-half minutes. Injury prevention is my goal.

Tapering: The two weeks prior to a 20km race, I start tapering. Two days before a race, I will do three 1/4-mile intervals or three 400-meter intervals to tune up my muscles. I only do the short distances just before a race.

Heart Rate Monitor vs Perceived Effort: I am a civil engineer and am inquisitive. I will try different training methods and evaluate them. For a while I trained with a heart rate monitor and I would evaluate the effort involved in specific heart rates. I have progressed to the point where I only use the monitor once in a while to check myself. I workout mostly on the basis of perceived effort. I know how my turnover affects my heart rate and how the speed of my arm swing affects it. I use perceived effort at all levels of training from my long, slow distance workouts to my intermediate and speed workouts.

CAMPS:

I find that camps give me new insights into training and technique. Everyone has a unique, different way of teaching the same thing. Camps give me the reassurance that what I am doing is correct, and they teach me something new. I think if anyone can go to a camp and come away with two, three or four ideas to use in their training or racing, they are way ahead. You will be taught dozens of things at a good camp. Some of them may not suit your style of training, but the few tips that do help make your time worthwhile.

The only downside I see in camps is that they are not long enough. Most of us are confined to weekends. There just is not enough time in two or two and one-half days. A week-long camp would really be great. However, most of us are working people and have to get back home for Monday.

COMPETITION

I consider myself a national competitor in the masters division. I try to do as many national races as I can from the 3km to the 25km, indoors and outdoors. These races give me goals all year.

My racing strategy is to break long races into smaller races. When I do a 20km race, I do not think of doing 20km. I break the race down into 5km or 2km or 1km races. I have an overall time that I want to make, and I figure out beforehand what my split times should be according to the course. If the 20km is on a track, I break the race into twelve 4-lap races. If it is on the road with a 2km loop, I break the race into ten 2km races. If I can find out where the 1km mark is on a 2km loop, I will break my race into twenty 1Km races.

By working to make a specific time each loop, I maintain control of my race. If I am five seconds fast, or if I am three seconds slow, I know how much I have to adjust for the next lap. Sometimes I get lost as to what my overall time is. I just know that I have completed the loop in the time I wanted, and then shift my focus completely to doing the next loop in the desired time.

I do not necessarily compete with the walkers in my age group. There are not many 50-year-olds who go my pace except for Don DeNoon who is always way out ahead of me. I usually check out the start line at a race to see who is there, and I pick out a few people who can pace me. I will try to stay with them or keep them in sight to keep me going.

In the last year, I have learned not to fly off the start line. I am being more conservative now and am taking it easier the first lap or two. Holding back at the start of a race is simply something you have to learn.

When I race, my drive is to be the best masters in the race. I am confident that I can be competitive, and that is what I want to be. I want to be up at the top. I set goals for myself that I can obtain and then strive to push beyond them in a race. I may have the goal of being the first overall masters as well as the goal of finishing at the top of my age group. If I have a bad race with a slow time, I may not be first overall, but I may still come in second in my age group.

I have been asked if I have always been competitive, and I explain it this way: When I started racing, I was very happy doing the shorter 3km and

5km distances. After the 5km at the Regional Championships in Raleigh, NC, Norm Frable asked me, "When are you going to do a man's race?" His question goaded me into training for the 20km. I thank Norm for that push.

When I met Don DeNoon, I was surprised to see that his stature and mine were similar. Don and I became friends just through racing. He taught me to go beyond what a 50-year-old was supposed to do. Because I was training with younger walkers, I did not know what the best 50-year-old times were. I did not know that I was walking just one minute or so off the American Age-Group Record.

In fact, I did not know there was such a thing as an age-group record until I raced the 5km at the Masters Outdoor Nationals in Provo, Utah in 1993. Don DeNoon was in the 5km with me. They kept announcing that he was on a record pace and I was just behind him. At the end of the race I thought, "Hey, I almost broke the record, too, and I finished second."

From Don I have learned that there is no age limit to what you can do. You can excel within the potential of who you are yourself. So that is what I have been doing. I have taken Don's enthusiasm and his spirit and focused on doing better for myself. I have gotten where I am today because I recognize no limits and will not recognize them.

MASTERS RACEWALKING

It is my view that this country has a few, good, young senior racewalkers, 39 and under. However, when you compare our masters racewalkers, 40 and over, to those of other countries, our masters are doing a lot better than our seniors in international competition. Some of our gold medal winning masters are in their 60s and 70s. There are a lot in their 40s and 50s, too.

Masters put their own time and money into training and into competing on the national and world levels. Count the individual and team medals Americans won in Miyazaki. There were an amazing 44 medals. Hardly a walker came back from Japan without a medal, and many were gold. That says it all for our masters racewalking program!

I try to encourage non-exercising men and women to give walking a try to help their fitness. Walking is a good way to get an aerobic workout. It is a good way to lose weight. You can do power walking just using your arms.

You do not have to straighten your legs to get a good workout. However, I encourage anyone who wants to walk fast to try racewalking.

Another plus to walking is that it gives a husband and wife an opportunity to participate in the same sport. My wife Kathy also racewalks which makes it great for me. We can go to races together and make it a vacation. I have talked with many masters athletes who do not have understanding at home. It makes it difficult for them, so I appreciate having an understanding wife.

In the four years I have been in serious competition, the people I have met and the people who I race against have become family. We go to races to meet each other and to see what is going on in each other's lives. I look at our racewalking community very much as a family, and I like it.

Don Denoon

Ray Funkhouser

Enrique Camarena

DON DENOON (M50)
RAY FUNKHOUSER (M40)
THE BEST OF COMPETITORS 1992-3

DON DENOON

I guess I was ahead of the times because when everyone was walking straight up and pulling with their heels, I knew I needed to lean forward and push with my toes.

I get out there and bust myself right from the start and see what I have left at the end. I do not hold anything back.

I Running-Walking Combination
II 1960s versus 1990s
III Nutrition
IV Masters Racewalking
In Action — Invitational Washington D.C.
Miyazaki — World Veterans Games

Don DeNoon is a runner who happens to be an extraordinary racewalker. Returning to the sport in 1992 after many years of absence, Don immediately made his presence well known among masters walkers. At age 49, he set 4 American records: 10km Championship in Niagara, 45:00 flat; 20km in Washington D.C., 1:36:09, 3000 meters indoors, 12:59 and outdoors, 12:47. At age 50, he set a 20km American record in Miyazaki, Japan, 1:34:55. A few of his outstanding 1994 times are: 20km National Invitational, Washington, D.C., in March, 1:33:38; 10km Championship, Niagara, NY, in July, 44:59; 5km National Masters Outdoor Championships Eugene, OR, in August, 21:55.5. Don became injured and did not race again until July 1995 at the World Veterans Games in Buffalo. He competed in the 5km and came in 3rd with a time of 24:01.

RUNNING-WALKING COMBINATION

I have never had a racewalk coach. I have never had anyone sit down and tell me what is right or wrong except for my wife. However, I do know how to develop athletes and I honestly believe that racewalkers need to train with running. They need to do all of their base work running, or the majority of it running. On the other hand, they need to do most of their technique training doing intervals at a track and at much higher accelerations than they do competing.

Years ago, I used a training ratio of 60/40, 60 percent running and 40 percent walking. When I really got into the heavy competitive racewalking season, the ratio would be 60 percent racewalking and 40 percent running. However, 100 percent of my racewalking was on the track doing intervals.

This past year I have been putting in 50 to 65 miles a week both running and walking. I run five days and I walk two days doing high speed, intense intervals on the track. The only disadvantage to this schedule is that my walking muscles have not adapted totally.

I have never had a bent knee problem. If I have ever received warnings, it has been because of being off the ground and going too fast. People who saw me walk last year, Alongi for one, commented that my technique is compatible with what is being taught today. Yet, my form has always been the same. I guess I was ahead of the times because when everyone was walking straight up and pulling with their heels, I knew I needed to lean forward and push with my toes. The only thing I would like to experiment with today is walking with short spikes in short, fast races. I think the spikes would give me a bit of an advantage. They would stabilize my foot because I push off so hard that sometimes I get some slippage.

NUTRITION

In 1992, a friend of mine persuaded me to try a drink called GO. GO is an amino acid drink invented by the man who came out with Gatorade. It has all the essential amino acids and is easy to digest. Because of its high protein content, the calories in GO assimilate more slowly in the body than carbohydrates. Put another way, you get longer lasting benefits from protein calories than you get from carbohydrate calories.

Maybe it is psychological, but after five days of drinking GO I had more energy than I ever imagined having. When I stopped the drink for a week, I could barely put one foot in front of the other. It took about three weeks to figure out what had happened. When I ordered another case, I picked right up again.

I have been in tune with my body almost from the day I started running at 13. I know how my body reacts to high stress and how it functions in different conditions. Since I started GO, I recover more quickly from my workouts. I also race strong because I have an abundance of energy. I take GO in place of my usual breakfast of fruit and cereal and seem to require less calories. I do not get hungry until after lunch time as the drink makes me feel full.

Other than GO, I eat a good ol' American diet. I love meat. I love milk and I drink nearly a quart a day.

1960s VERSUS 1990s

In the 1960s, people who did not exercise were intimidated by those who did. If you were working out along the roads, they would swerve into you with their cars or throw beer cans, coke cans or water at you. There were so few people who trained, it was not an acceptable thing to do. Today, exercise is more generally accepted by the public.

People are more curious today. If I am out on the track doing an interval session, onlookers want to know what I am doing and will come up to talk. In the '60s, they would look at you as if you were a leper. You were considered a strange person and someone to avoid.

On the other hand, racewalkers had a lot of crowd appeal as a novelty in the indoor circuit during the '60s. People would be laughing their heads off as we warmed up. When the race started, they would soon get caught up in the competition and start cheering. When I broke the world mile record in 1966, the crowd was screaming and yelling.

Today, walkers are flocking to local runs and walks. Sometimes I give short five-minute clinics right before a walk and people really listen. Racewalking is easy to teach if you know how to teach it. I give instructions about the rules and then explain how to abide by the rules. I tell people that they need to think as a jogger, and then show them how to shift from a jog to a racewalk. I show them how they must straighten their legs and use their hips. After giving them some time to visualize themselves both jogging and racewalking, I have them do it.

I think it is much easier for people to learn to racewalk from jogging than from street walking. It is much easier for them to get the mental concept of how to drive and how to push.

MASTERS RACEWALKING

Masters racewalking is great because it provides an opportunity for people to reach goals in athletic pursuit. Goals are what make life go. When I was 48, my goal was to try to make the Olympic Trials. It kept me going. Other people have the goal of winning their age-group division in a particular race, or of beating a masters record. People can grab hold of such goals at any age and become physically fit and mentally alive.

Probably one of the most ego deflating things that happened to me was to win the National 10km Masters Championship in Niagara in 1992 because I admitted that I was "old." I beat all the "old" people. Up to then, I had been competing against the kids and was one of the kids. It was a reality check for me to compete against those my own age as well as against masters younger than me.

My present goal is to see what I can do. I am nine pounds lighter, and I need races to find out what's in me. Instead of being a 45-minute 10km walker, I think I could be a 42-minute 10km walker if I can keep up the same training intensity. I finished sixth in the Niagara open division. Maybe, I am fantasizing, but I see myself as being able to win a national championship in the open division.

I am an extremely focused athlete and have always been. I do not think I have ever met a competitor who is more focused than I am except for Mary Decker. When I am on the starting line getting ready to race, I do not think anything else goes through my mind except driving toward the finish line.

IN ACTION

The experiences people have competing are timeless. Competitors have faced, are facing and will face similar challenges as long as they enter races. The racing comments of Don DeNoon are from 1993, but their insights will always be current. The following was recorded after the National Invitational Racewalk in Washington, D.C., March 1993. Don's 20km time was 1:32:21. Ray's was 1:33:20.

Ray and I were pretty much together at the 10km marker. Then he pulled ahead of me. I did not feel very good at that particular time, but I did not want to let go. I think I was probably 20 meters back at the end of 12km. At 13km, I decided to try to surge for one-half mile to see if I could break him. I came up and he would not let me pass. I waited for a good open spot, and then I sprinted by him and just kept going. I heard him back there for quite a while. He did not give up, but I just kept pressing and it was another kilometer before I could not hear him breathing.

I felt pretty good again at this point. I had not received any warnings and I tried to get my center of gravity a little higher to make it a little easier. I think I was too cautious and trying to be too legal at the beginning of the race, and was putting too much pressure on my lower back, quads and hamstrings by trying to stay too low. I think that fatigued me.

When you lower your center of gravity, you lower your arms and drive your heels more into the ground. This action puts more stress on your lower body and is tiring. Raising your arms and pushing off with your toes lifts your center of gravity and makes it easier to walk.

During the race, my 2km times varied between 8:40 and 9:30. At the end of the race, I was tired. My cadence was not fast and the length of my stride was probably too long. Though I took a lot of the pressure off my lower body by raising my center of gravity, I did not have the turnover. If I had done it earlier, I probably would not have been as fatigued mid-race.

A lot of people have said to me, "You go out too fast." I say, "You never know what you are capable of doing unless you go out there and pay the price early." That has been a strategy of mine ever since the day I stepped on the track. I get out there and bust myself right from the start and see what I have left at the end. I don't hold anything back. I was at 22:05 for 5km.

One of the things that enhanced my race after I passed Ray is that I started keying, not on the person in front of me, but on two or three people ahead. I was constantly pulling on someone who was 50 to 100 meters in front of me. I just stared at their backs and they kept pulling me. As I got close, I would refocus on someone else 100 meters out. This way I was able to keep myself mentally alert.

Recorded after the World Veterans Games, Miyazaki, Japan, October 1993. Don was first overall and first in his age division of M50 with a time of 1:34:55.

The race went off at 12:30 midday, and the heat and humidity were strong factors affecting everyone. There was a massive group at the start line because the course was narrow. I think it was only nine meters wide and that included both going out and coming back. About 200 to 300 meters out, the course funneled down to about 4.5 meters. It was set up like an English traffic course so we were walking on the left going out and coming back. It made it somewhat tough on the turns because in the U.S. our orientation is always to turn to the left, not to the right. Besides that, the turns were miserably tight, a traffic cone type, making it necessary to slow down.

At the beginning of the race, the guy from Columbia took off like he was shot out of a canon, and I just watched him go. I was in second place. At 600 meters, I went right by him. When we got to the first turn at the 1000 meter point, I could see everybody behind me and at that particular stage, I had about a 40 meter lead. There were four 40-year-olds right there in a big pack. I was really feeling good and just said to myself, "Hey, go for it! It's what you want. Go for it!" So I kept pressing until I built up about a two minute lead by the 15km marker.

At this point, I made a cautious decision. There was one area on the course where either the same judge or a couple of judges showed me the paddle for loss of contact. I kept looking at the DQ board as I went by every 2500 meters and at 10,000 meters, one red card went up. At 15km I said to myself, "Why screw it up right now and keep pressing like I am." So I dropped my center of gravity a bit, concentrated on technique and watched where the competition was at each turn to make sure they were not catching me. The guys in the pack behind me were competing against each other and put a big surge on the last 2500 meters, but I knew where they were all along and just eased in. It felt really good to go across the finish line.

RAY FUNKHOUSER

Weight training has helped my technique in that I am able to hold the proper posture for good, efficient walking for longer periods.

Ray Funkhouser was a member of the Men's National Racewalking Team for five years. In 1992, he set American masters records (M40) in the 20km, 1:29:35; the 10km, 43:26; Indoor 3km, 12:43. In 1993, he improved his indoor 3km time to 12:25. The following is taken from interviews held in 1992 and early 1993.

RUNNER TO RACEWALKER

I was a distance runner through high school and college. After that I got into road racing. The summer of 1978, I was running in a summer track series and decided to enter the walk. For the next two years, I trained as a runner, but when there was a racewalk somewhere, I would go and walk.

On January 1, 1980 I made a New Year's resolution. I decided to make the full switch to racewalking. I realized that running and racewalking involved different muscles, and that I had to train with the proper technique if I ever wanted to excel in racewalking.

By 1984, I won the National 20km championship and came in seventh in the Olympic Trials in Los Angeles. This put me on the National 20km Team and I represented the United States at the first Pan American Racewalking Cup in Bucamaranga, Columbia. I was on the Men's National Team five years.

FACTORS IN COMEBACK SUCCESS

DIET CHANGES

There are several changes I have made in my life style that have assisted my comeback. One of the most important is that I have changed my eating habits. I really watch my fat intake and limit myself to about 50 grams a day. I stay away from anything that is fried or has a cream sauce. When I pick up a container of food, I do not look so much at the calories as I do the fat content. At the same time, I eat everything else. I still eat meat. I just make sure when I eat meat that it is lean. I eat a lot of chicken, turkey, fish and pasta.

WEIGHT LIFTING

The second change I have made is to start on a year-round program of lifting weights three times a week. I am on a program that is written out for me so I do not have to think about it. I go into the gym and I follow the written workout for that day. It tells me exactly what weights to use and how many sets and reps to do. Then every four weeks, I take a test and send my programmer the results. He adjusts my program according to my test results for the next month.

My program uses periodization so that I will peak for my big races. It alternates between a rest phase which my programmer calls an activation phase, a maximum strength phase where I increase my weights with very few reps, and an endurance phase where I do high numbers of reps with lighter weights. The endurance phase gets my muscles used to working in a fatigued state.

The weight training has helped my racewalking technique in that I am able to hold the proper posture for good, efficient walking for longer periods. My upper body strength is probably greater than it ever has been in my life. I would say for the majority of walkers, upper body strength and abdominal strength are weak areas and that their walking would improve by strengthening these muscles.

The only time I cut back on the weight training is if a big race is coming up. Otherwise, I lift weights three times a week in addition to my racewalking workouts.

WORKOUT PARTNER

Finally, I have a training partner for the first time in my life, Phyllis Hansen. When we set times to workout, I know I have to be there because someone is depending on me. Training on your own leaves latitude. You can get busy doing something at work and say, "OK, I will go out a little later today." Before you know it, the day has passed and you have skipped the workout because of the day's pressures.

I am also coaching Phyllis. Coaching has caused me to spend a lot more time reading the racewalking literature. Analyzing what she is doing makes me analyze what I am doing. We are using a heart rate monitor during our track workouts which has been very helpful. It has taken me a few months to really get used to it. The numbers were always very interesting, but I did not always know what they meant.

When Phyllis and I are in what I call our "real training phase," we do intervals at the track once a week. We will do some repeat 400's and repeat 1km's. The pace we go depends on the race ahead. If my goal is to do a 20km under 1:30:00, I prepare by walking 1km's slightly under the pace needed for that time. This pace is slightly under 4:30.

We use local races for a second speed workout a week. There are a lot of road races where we live in New Jersey. We do not taper down for them, but actually train through them. So these races never interrupt our training.

Handicapping: Sometimes I give Phyllis a handicap based on the 1km time I want her to walk and the 1km time I want to walk so theoretically we finish together. I always have my work cut out for me as she does not want me to catch her. This kind of handicapping is a very effective way of working out with someone who cannot go as fast as you can.

One day a week we do an "overdistance" workout. If Phyllis has a 10km race coming up, we will walk one hour and twenty minutes. On those days, I will try to get up early enough to walk another hour by myself. I have never been a high mileage person, even when I was a runner. I am more concerned with the quality of the workout.

I usually do not record miles in my training log. I just record the length of time and the effort made during a workout. In other words, I write down whether I worked out one hour at race pace, or one and one-half hours at a 80 percent effort. A ball park figure of mileage would be between 40 and 50 miles a week.

IN ACTION

Post race comments after the March 1993 Washington Invitational where Ray finished just behind Don DeNoon. Ray's time: 1:33:20.

Based on my training, I am satisfied with today's race. Last year was much different. (In March 1992, Ray raced to qualify for the 20km Olympic Trials. The qualifying time was 1:30:00, and he finished in 1:29:35.) This year I did more indoor meets. To prepare for them, I concentrated on speed work and did no long distance.

Today's 20km is the farthest I have walked this year. The way the masters 1993 schedule is set up makes a long season with the World Veteran's Games in October. If I trained to be in peak 20km shape this early in the year, I know I would not be able to keep it up. This race has served the purpose of letting me know where my 20km time is and what needs to be done.

As for the indoor season, I walked faster than I have for a number of years. I did a 3000-meter in 12:25, and three 3000- meter races under 12:40. I had a 6:14 mile at Milrose. Now I will start building for the outdoor season. *(As it turned out, Ray was not able to go to Miyazaki for the World Veterans Games.)*

ENRIQUE CAMARENA (M45)

Breathing correctly is primary to the racewalking technique. It is part of the discipline of good technique.

If you do get injured, just walking at a comfortable, brisk pace allows your injury to heal and maintains your endurance.

I The Warm Up - Stretches & breathing exercises
II The Workout
III Nutrition
IV Mental Preparation & Race Strategy

Enrique Camarena (M45) walks for the Southern Cal Walkers. He won gold medals in his age division in the 5km, 23:26.8 and 20km, 1:43.51 in 1994 at Eugene in the Masters Outdoor Nationals. He won the Los Angeles Marathon, March 5, 1995 with a time of 4:15:41, and on St. Patrick's Day walked the 20km in 1:43.20. He came in 6th in the 5km at the World Veterans Games in Buffalo with a time of 24:18

AN OLYMPIC WAGER

I became attracted to racewalking because I was getting tired of running. I was training to qualify for the Boston Marathon when the Olympics came to Los Angeles in 1984. I saw some of the great racewalkers of the world competing. As I was watching, I said to myself, "If a Mexican walker gets the gold medal in the 50km, I will start racewalking. If an American wins the Olympic marathon, then I will qualify for Boston." The American did not win and the Mexican did. That is how I got started racewalking.

It was fairly easy for me to learn to racewalk because I had the endurance of running. I always tell my running friends if they get tired of running, they should go into racewalking.

THE WARM-UP

The warm-up is an important part of a good workout as racewalking depends on flexibility and strength.

Upper body exercises: On the weekends, I start my long distance workouts with 15 to 20 minutes of exercises and stretches. I start with windmills and then do a swimming type of arm stroke I learned from Hausleber in Mexico. It is a forward stroke and starts somewhat like the butterfly stroke except that I cross my arms as I bring them down in front of me. It is good for shoulder and torso flexibility. Doing this swim stroke walking uphill is good for hip flexibility.

A good standing hip stretch starts by crossing your legs with your feet pointing forward. Keeping your rear leg straight, lean sideways dangling your arms over your rear foot. Your body forms an arc from your ankle to the top of your head.

Breathing exercises: Usually I do breathing exercises walking, but they can be done standing. I do not worry about my pace. As I raise my arms over my head, I inhale and hold my breath as long as it is comfortable. I lower my arms as I exhale. It is important not to make a big effort inhaling or exhaling. You should stay relaxed and natural. Breathing exercises help you to expand your lungs and to strengthen their support muscles.

Breathing correctly is primary to the racewalking technique. It is part of the discipline of good technique. When I race my breathing is completely controlled. As long as you breath with your mouth closed, you can maintain control.

For example, suppose I am racewalking a 10km. I get to 8km and I am breathing quickly. I need a second wind. The first thing I do is focus on my shoulders and arms to see if there is tension. If there is, I take a deep breath in and out, almost like a quick sigh. As I breath out, my upper body relaxes right away. It helps my hip rotation and my energy picks up.

On almost any course, there is a spot where there is an opportunity to get your wind back. It may be a very slight downhill. You use this spot to recuperate, to take a deep breath, exhale and say "Go" to yourself. If you know the course and know the best spot, always take advantage of it. Quick recovery is what you learn when you do 100-meter sprints.

THE WORKOUT

The workouts I do are similar to the Mexicans' workouts; the only difference is I do not swim. My workout week starts on the weekend. Saturday and Sunday are for long distance to build endurance. The pace is moderate, no pushing. A flat course is best, but rolling hills are okay. The way I train for a 10km and 20km is pretty much the same. The following training schedule assumes that a walker is in good physical condition. It is for a 10km and 20km race.

Sat. 10km— 6 miles: 3 just walking, 3 running or jogging
20km—10 miles: 5 just walking, 5 running or jogging

Sun.

	Walking,	running	racewalking
10km—10 miles:	2	3	5
20km—14-16 mi:	3	5	8

Mon. Speed workout racewalking 3 miles at 5km speed.

Tues. 6 miles, easy steady pace: 3 miles at 45-50 secs. per mile over 10km pace; 3 miles at 30 secs. per mile over 10km pace.

Wed. Speed workout - intervals for 3 miles.
4 x 100m repeats racewalking full out followed by 20-40 seconds of easy walking for recovery.
2 x 400m repeats, 20-40 seconds recovery.
3 x 800m repeats, 20-40 seconds recovery.
The shorter the distance the faster you go. The recovery interval can be lengthened for the age and condition of a walker. It can be adjusted to heart rate or breathing, whatever works best for the individual. The purpose is to build the body's capacity and endurance for speed.

Thus. 6 miles at an easy steady pace, similar to Tuesday.

Fri. Day off. Relaxation. Complete rest.

A speed workout for the 20km may consist of 10 1-km repeats. How fast varies. Now suppose I am training with a guy who wants to walk around 1:35:00. We start with an 8:00 per mile pace. By the 6th repeat, the pace is 7:40 and by the final repeat we might do 7:30. In kilometers that would be 4:55, 4:50, 4:45, 4:40.

You have to be very careful not to injure yourself doing speed. The moment you feel that your body is telling you something — one little sharp pain in your hip or shoulder — slow down. If you go back to a 4:55 or even 4:59 pace, you do not have to worry because you are still within your workout.

The Mexican walkers have strict discipline. They do so well because of their discipline. They do their long distance on weekends and they do two speed workouts and two steady workouts during the week. Right after working out, they go in a pool for 30 minutes to swim and have fun. They swim to build their shoulders, to build lung power and to relax. I feel plain walking is a good substitute for swimming.

Racewalking takes a lot of work. Obviously, you get tired. If you racewalk constantly without other types of workouts, the intensity can lead to injuries. By doing some of the miles just walking on the weekends, you allow your body to recuperate.

When I say "just walking," I mean walking at a natural, brisk, comfortable pace. If you do get injured, plain walking at a brisk pace allows your injury to heal while maintaining your endurance. For example, if you have almost recovered from a hamstring injury and only have occasional twinges of pain, you insure complete recovery by continuing to just walk during your regular workouts. When you no longer have any pain, you can start racewalking.

You should mix plain, brisk walking with racewalking for as long as you live. How far you just walk depends on the distance of your workouts. If a workout is 5 to 10 miles, then 2 or 3 miles is good. If the workout is longer for endurance, you might brisk walk more miles. Endurance is first and then speed.

NUTRITION

I eat my Mexican food. My body is used to spicy foods. I eat beans and rice. I really am not afraid of eating anything because I burn off everything in my training. I take good vitamins and drink a lot of Carbofuel, a carbohydrate drink. It comes in powder form and is sold in health food stores.

You put three scoops of Carbofuel in eight ounces of water. The scoop comes with the powder. I find that if I drink the carbofuel before and after a race or workout, I recuperate faster. When I do my races or workouts, I recuperate in 20 to 30 minutes.

I drink water during the race. You do not need to drink anything special if you take the Carbofuel. For a long distance like the marathon, I take double the amount of Carbofuel before starting. Ideally, you would have someone along the course and would take a second carbohydrate drink mid-race.

There is a little trick to taking water during a race. If I do not feel like drinking, I just take a sip because water can get stuck in your stomach. On short distances, you do not need water. If you have taken something like Carbofuel before the race, sipping water is okay.

There is another drink that I take every day for breakfast. It is very nutritious and it tastes good. You blend 8-10 ounces of milk, 2 tablespoons of molasses, 1 egg yoke, 1 banana (or strawberries), and 4 teaspoons Brewer's yeast. Another drink that I take on weekends has a long recipe. It is a vegetable drink with lemon tea and yogurt that is made in a blender. The recipe is: One leaf of lettuce, one leaf of green cabbage, one bunch of celery, one bunch of parsley, one tomato, one medium carrot, several leaves of spinach, one medium beet, four radishes, one medium cucumber, one bell pepper with the seeds removed, 1/4 of a purple onion, 1 head of garlic, juice of six lemons, 1 cup plain yogurt (lemon or orange flavored is okay), 1 cup lemon tea.

Blend all vegetables with the lemon juice. Add the yogurt and tea last. As it takes a while to make, you can drink one-half on Saturday and one-half on Sunday. If you take this drink for two weekends in a row, it is good for the immune system.

MENTAL PREPARATION

As soon as I start training for a 20km race, I set my mind on the race. For example: You will find that when you get home after a workout, there are moments when you really feel like relaxing. Take advantage of these moments. Do not let them pass. Sit down, relax your body and let your mind go. These are valuable moments of preparation.

The morning of the 20km race, my mind is set not to be tense. If my race is at 8 a.m., I get up two to three hours ahead. I am thinking about relaxing and keeping completely relaxed. Mentally, I am telling myself: "I am going to do my race. I am not going to follow the others. This is my race. I have worked out hard for this race. I have my endurance. I have done my speed work. I have everything I need for my race."

My mind is on racing. I am not worrying about the conditions. If I have to drive to the race, my mind is on the race. If I am staying in a dorm and walking to the race, my mind is on the race. I meet people, "Good morning," but my mind is on the race.

I visualize the course as part of my prerace preparation. When I am at the start line of a good course, I am focusing on the far end of the loop. If I am racing on a track, my mind is four or five laps ahead when the race starts. I am always thinking ahead when I am racing. I may be competing at a particular spot, but I am thinking ahead. I am also always telling myself to relax.

I learned to focus ahead of my competitors when I was running. I got to know many good runners at the weekend races. Before a race, some would come up and say things like, "Hey, I'm going to beat you." They were trying to get hold of my mind. But by focusing ahead of them, their words had no power.

Sometimes I will have the goal of beating someone. But again, you see, my mind is already set ahead. That is where training counts — endurance, speed and breathing.

I have been experiencing a lot of things that I never thought would happen to me the last few years. The more I discipline what I am doing, the more I learn. Everything comes together. Discipline, mind set, relaxing and racing. That is why I never get afraid that someone is going to beat me. If they can go faster, fine; but my mind is already set on what I am going to do.

By being able to set goals and achieve them, competition builds self-confidence and self-esteem. When you commit yourself to a training program and discipline yourself to do it, it is good for all the rest of your life. Sports gives you a chance to prove yourself to yourself.

ED KOUSKY (M50)

Only in masters sports do you find people looking forward to getting to the next age group.

For the person who loses focus from time to time, cautions serve an important and helpful function.

I Racewalking as compared to running
II Training
III Nutrition
IV Camps

Ed Kousky (M50) is another runner turned racewalker. In 1980, he was in a sky diving accident and underwent knee surgery. He ripped two ligaments, the posterior cruciate and medial collateral of one knee. He continued to run after this surgery and was quite successful until 1989 when his knee began giving him problems. After two more surgeries in 1990 and 1992, he turned to racewalking. Since that time, Ed has won several medals in his age group, his latest being a silver in the 20km at the World Veterans Games in Buffalo with a time of 1:51:33.

RACEWALKING COMPARED TO RUNNING

After running for so many years, my biggest challenge was learning the racewalking technique. The basics of training for racewalking and running are pretty much the same. You do distance to build a base, you do ladders and you do repeat 400's or 800's. Similarly, a runner's attitude toward competition applies to racewalkers. Articles on mental preparation and race strategy apply to both sports.

Racewalking's unique difference is the need for proper technique. In running, you can run any which way you want and not get disqualified. You can crawl across the finish line. This is not true of racewalking. Proper technique remains essential from start to finish.

Successful racewalkers also have to stay focused for longer periods of time than runners. They need to concentrate during training as well as during competition. I tend to daydream when I am racewalking and this is risky because of my knee injury. When I get tired, I lose the feel of my right knee. Consequently, I must concentrate all the harder on the mechanics of keeping it straight and legal. Only by focusing on doing the hip rotation and footwork correctly can I feel reasonably sure that my leg is straight.

At the same time, racewalking works for my particular knee problem. Though I have lost cartilage and have shortened ligaments, the muscles around my knee are strong. The problem of bone rubbing bone does not bother me when I racewalk because of the straight leg coming through. In fact, proper technique keeps my bones in alignment. In addition, there isn't the jarring that comes with running with its heavy-footed impact on the ground. Racewalking is just an easy, heel to toe, straight legged gait.

TRAINING

The Masters Outdoor Nationals and the WAVA championships are only three months away and I have to start adding mileage to my training. I have been working on a base and have done a couple of local races, but I need to get more focused. If you train to run a marathon, your longest run will be a 22-miler. If you train to racewalk 20km, you train for 25km.

Up to now, I have been doing mostly 10km's or 8-milers. I need to be doing 10km on the short days and 25km on the long days. I will be gradually increasing distance for the next two and one-half months.

My objective is to be physically and mentally ready to do the best I can. I do not do a lot of deep breathing exercises as some do. I do not do much visualization before a race, but I do some.

Next year, I will be 55 which will put me in a new age division at the Indoor Nationals. I am looking forward to being the "youngest." Only in masters sports do you find men and women looking forward to getting into the next age group. Competition keeps older athletes thinking and staying young.

CAMPS

Weekend camps benefit those who can afford to fly to them and can afford the time off from work. What I like about camps is that you are with a group of racewalkers who are all trying to become better. They are trying to improve their techniques and to learn better training methods. When campers go back home, they pass information along to others. I feel that the more camps there are and the more people attend them, the more and better racewalkers there will be across the United States.

Besides the expense of camps, there are a few other possible problems. You cannot always count on the weather being nice. It can be miserable. Sometimes, there is not enough personnel present at a camp to give instruction. You may be expecting to work with a specific coach and find that he or she is off competing somewhere.

Where I live in Oregon, I train by myself. There are lots of runners, but no racewalkers. What I would like, and I think everyone would like, is to have a group of walkers for regular workouts and a coach to check on technique once a week. It would be very helpful.

Camps provide a good alterative for those like me. However, most camps mix beginners with advanced walkers. Since I have gone to several, I am becoming more selective about the clinics and camps I attend. There comes a time when you need to look for a camp or clinic that will be oriented to your level of ability. Ideally, there would be beginning, intermediate and advanced camps. As the numbers of racewalkers increase, perhaps these divisions may become feasible.

NUTRITION

Like runners, I watch what I eat and when I eat it. I do the same with what I drink. If I have an early morning race, I do not eat breakfast. I eat a good meal the night before, but do not do anything special like carboloading. I stay pretty much to my regular diet. I do not take vitamins or special supplements. Every so often, I will try some miracle concoction, but have not noticed that it makes any difference. One time I tried a supplement that was supposed to increase energy, endurance and P.R.'s. The recommended dose was six a day. All it did was turn my urine a golden color. I did not notice anything else.

I am not a vegetarian so I eat lean meat. I do not eat as much fish as I probably should. I eat a lot of chicken, turkey, rice and potatoes. I like vegetables and fresh fruits. I eat most foods in moderation and will eat a Whopper or Big Mac once in a while. I do not eat much dessert. I look at the fat grams in foods and stay away from cookies, crackers and such. With all the nutrition information available, it is easy to avoid foods with a high fat content.

If a person can find out if he or she has deficiencies, then I can see supplementing with professional advice. For example, someone may need a calcium tablet or iron pill. It is probably okay to take a multivitamin just to be on the safe side. Basically I think people should eat in moderation, and as long as they are exercising, they will do okay.

JUDGING

I think it is very important for judges to adhere to the recommendation of giving competitors cautions before turning in a red card. I understand that there are times when it is not possible, but most of the time it is possible.

What we are trying to do in Eugene is take the obvious illegal walker out of a race. On the other hand, for the person who loses focus from time to time, cautions serve an important and helpful function. In a race last year, one of my friends in my age group was trying to pass me. I was ahead of him, but he came on strong toward the end of the race. He was clearly lifting. The judge put the paddle in his face and he backed off. The caution served its proper purpose. My friend went back to being legal and finished second. This is an example of good judging.

The rules recommend one caution and then a red card. It helps fair competition to follow this process. It gives every competitor an opportunity to self-correct so he or she can stay in the race. There have been some races when I have not received a caution and have been surprised to discover I have a red card.

I would also like to see judges position themselves where there are no tricky curves, ramps, tight turnarounds or whatever. For instance, unless a walker slows way down at a sharp turnaround, maintaining straight knees is nearly impossible. It is not fair to give a red card under this condition. The walker is not intentionally bending his or her knees. The rule violation is simply a probability caused by competitive speeds at that particular spot on that course.

As a walker with a knee problem, obviously I would like to see the straight knee rule modified for older folks whom we are trying to encourage to racewalk. The debate about leniency is ongoing. One group says, "If walkers cannot straighten their knee, they shouldn't racewalk." The other group says, "If they can't keep a straight leg because of arthritis or injury, some accommodation should be made."

If athletes are obviously trying to use proper racewalking technique and they are not gaining an advantage on other competitors, I can see ignoring a slightly bent knee. This would apply only to older age groups. On the other hand, if it is very obvious that a few walkers are illegal, they should be DQ'ed. They need to learn about proper technique and how to walk legally.

In my opinion proper discretion was used at the Reno Masters Indoor National Championships. An older woman was competing indoors for the first time. It was obvious that she was trying very, very hard to stay legal. The judges recognized her effort, and she was allowed to finish the race and win a medal. No one was a loser because of her. In fact, everyone was a winner as the sport kept the enthusiasm and participation of an improving older athlete.

Ed Kousy

L to R: Bill Pender, Norm Frable, Jack Bray, Max Green

MAX GREEN (M60)

Once I get warmed up, I feel as limber as I ever was, and though the maximum volume of oxygen decreases with age, training counters this pretty well.

A fact not to be overlooked in making P.R.'s is the importance of having good people in a race.

I Training
With Partners, Age factor, Tips for New Masters
II Racing
Turku, Miyazaki with Jack Bray

Max Green, M60, holds numerous American records. He started to race in his early 50s with Frank Alongi as his coach, and within two years was establishing Single-Age Best Performances and USATF Age-Group Records. His records include: (M55, M60) 5km Track, (M55) 5km Road, (M55, M60) 10km, 20km; (M55) 15km, 25km, 40km & 50km. In July of 1995 (M60), Max won two gold medals at the Masters Outdoor Nationals in E. Lansing. His 5km time was 25:36. His 20km was 1:54:24. At the Buffalo World Veterans Games one week later, he won a silver medal in the 20km at 1:53:19 and a bronze medal in the 5km at 25:23.11.

TRAINING

PARTNERS *The following is taken from an interview with Max in June 1990 after a spectacular record setting season. He was 58-years-old.*

My secret in making the 20km record this year was working out with two young ladies who can walk much faster than I can. I trained with Zofia Wolan and her friend, Alicia. Their consistency put social pressure on me to go out every day even when it was five degrees and snowy or slushy.

I put in about 70 to 75 kilometers a week with them. Three to four times a week, I would do a reasonably fast 15km as the girls were doing 15km's every day. I walked under a 6:00 per kilometer pace those days. Nothing super duper, but always pretty good. We gradually worked our times down as the winter progressed. I did not train hard every day. Some days I would do an easy 10km at a 6:30 per kilometer pace. Things can heal at that speed.

By training with Zofia and Alicia, I did not have to be concerned about my pace. If I started falling back, I would start to think, "Am I too tired? Am I too old? Or am I doing some bad technique?" I would then start catching up. This gave me some immediate feedback and incentive to improve. If you train by yourself, you have no gauge. You may try hard to walk with good technique, but you do not immediately see its effects as I did when the distance began to close between Zofia and me.

Training with the women led to some of my best race times. In April I did my fastest 20km ever. Two weeks after that I did a 5km in 24:36 which is not my best, but it is good. The next day, I did a 10km in 50:11, again not my best time, but okay. One week later at the Southeastern Regional Masters Championship, Raleigh, NC, I walked a 20km in 1:46:34 which was my best 20km for a year.

However, my strength ran out. My legs were hurting in Raleigh, and I found out later that they were bruised. Little muscle tears probably caused the bruises. It was nothing serious. My legs have loosened up, but I think I am too old to have four hard races in four weeks like that.

AGING

Once I get warmed up, I feel as limber as I ever was, and though the maximum volume of oxygen intake decreases with age, training counters this pretty well. In Raleigh it was not my lungs that gave out. My legs were shot. I do not think my legs can go as fast now even when I am in my best shape. I am not going to get another best 5km or 10km.

My best 10km was four years ago when I was 54. I walked it in 49:56, so I am off 15 seconds four years later. My best 5km was 3 years ago at 24:16. I am off 20 seconds. I think I could have done a faster 5km this year if I had not just done a 20km. I think my technique has improved to offset the slowing process.

There are three things which Frank Alongi has been after me to correct:

(1) My feet. When I walk regularly, my feet splay out like ducks' feet. It is a family trait, but it is an inefficient way to walk fast. When you try to

push, you push off the sides of your toes rather than pushing straight back with them. I have been trying to turn my toes in so my feet point front.

(2) Knee lift. Tapes of my walking show that I have a tendency to lift my knee too high when the leg is coming forward. This wastes energy so I have been trying to keep my knees lower.

(3) Neck. Another problem is that I tend to bend my neck so my head hangs down. I am trying to hold my head up and still continue to lean from the ankles.

NEW MASTERS WALKERS

It is important to work on technique, but not so much that you never try to go fast. I think new walkers should try to go fast some of the time just to get the feeling of going fast, even if they lose technique and get in the air. It is hard to walk fast, and I think it is important to get the feeling. I do not think any coach would agree, but it is the advice I would give.

RACING

IN ACTION

The Jack Mortland Race, April 1990 when Max (M55) set a 20km American Age-Group Record at 1:43:41.

A fact not to be overlooked in making P.R.'s is the importance of having good people in a race. Besides being in good condition for the 20km at the Jack Mortland race, Victor Sipes, John Elwarner and I walked together during the first 10km. John led a fair amount of the time. At the 10km mark, Victor eased off. About 12.5km, I heard John breathing a little hard, and I knew that I was feeling pretty good. Looking at the clock, I saw that I had a chance of making an Age-Group Record as well as a 58-year-old record for 15km. I thought, "I'm going to pour it on for one more lap and then if I feel bad, at least I have something for the winter's training."

In the 7th lap, the next to the last lap, I realized Gary Morgan had not lapped me. I ordinarily might fall off pace some at this point in a race, but I realized Gary was not having a good race. I thought, "It looks like he might not catch me, so I'm not going to let him." At the beginning of the 8th lap, I realized I might beat the 20km record and decided to go as hard as possible. I was spurred on by the thought, "Let's see if I can do it."

There were many reasons I did well in that 20km. Besides my training and excellent competitors, the course was dead flat. There was not any wind and the temperature was in the 40's. Everything was in place for a good race.

1991 & 1993 WORLD VETERANS GAMES

TRAINING FOR TURKU

From an interview in the spring of 1991 when Max was training for The World Veterans Games in Turku, Finland.

I am doing about 80 kilometers a week. I try to do one 20km a week under a 6:00 per kilometer pace, and one set of 3km intervals at about a 5:10 to 5:15 per kilometer pace. Another day, I do a set of 10 1km's or 5 2km's — the 1km's down around 5:00 and the 2km's as close to the 1km pace as possible. These are three hard days. Two or three other days, I will try doing 15 kilometers. If I am tired I will walk over a 6:00 per kilometer pace. If I am feeling good, I will walk under a 6:00 per kilometer pace.

Earlier in the year, I was trying to do 20km's and 18km's moderately hard, averaging around a 5:35 pace which sounds easy until you try to do it every day. It is easy for one or two days, but by the third day, you feel tired. Because of the demands of my job, I did not have the energy to keep this level of training up. I find it is better doing intervals.

My goal at the World Veterans Games is 1:43:30 in the 20km. That is faster than my 1:43:41 last year, but I have been without injury longer and have been able to train without serious interruptions. I did the 1:43:41 after training about 3 1/2 months. This year, I started in January and will be training into July. It does not mean I will better my time, but I have some hope.

The competition will be hard. I am likely to be beaten by three or four guys. I cannot say all of their names. There is a Bob Gardner from Australia who is a former Olympian. He just turned 55 and walked a 20km in 1:41:56. I would suspect that he has a good chance of winning. There is a Fin and a Russian who are 55 and walked around 1:43:00 at the European Veterans Games last year. Also, there is an Englishman, David Stevens, who is fast, but his times right now are not as good as they should be because he was hurt last summer. I think if I could get a 1:43:30, I might get a medal. Someone can be sick or hurt. Every competitor has the same kind of troubles.

Jack Bray, of course, is out to beat me and I hope he does some time, but I certainly am not going to give it to him. His times are as good as mine, and I am not going to be first every time we meet. That is not possible. You have seen the Age- Graded ratings put out by "National Masters News". You can see that the 20km times get slower each year. Jack and I at 58 and 59 will be racing 55- and 56-year-olds.

Jack is always optimistic. We have different philosophies. He thinks if he says that he will do it, he will do it. I like saying I did it after I did it.

I do not know what I can do in the 5km in Turku. I did a couple of 5km's this year at 24:57 and 24:58, but I was not doing any intervals, just distance training.

IN ACTION AT TURKU, FINLAND, 1991 (M55)

Max (at 59-years) won the Bronze medal in the 20km with a time of 1:46:34. He did not medal in the 5km, but had a very respectable 24:23.9.

For much of the 20km race, I followed Sigurds Irbe who is a Latvian. He was listed as a Russian, but when he signed in, he substituted Latvia and wore a shirt with Latvia on it. He was fourth in the 5km earlier in the week, beating me substantially with a time of 24:03.

Before the race Dave Stevens, who finished second in the 20km, told me that Irbe was on the 50km Russian team at one time. I decided I would try to follow him. This worked well for about 10km. We got our splits at 5km, and my time was 19 seconds slower than I planned, 26:19 rather than 26:00 flat. I sped up and he did, too. He had quite a few people along the course coaching him. We went through the 10km point at 52:06 which was close to a 1:44.00. Then he faltered badly, so I went by him.

The next person was a New Zealander, Maurice Hinton. When I passed him, I was in third place. Dave and the first place walker were considerably ahead of me. They were going under 1:43 and I did not really try to catch them. I knew I had third if nothing happened, so I settled for safe.

IN ACTION AT MIYAZAKI, JAPAN, 1993, M60.

Max won the Gold Medal in the 20km with a time of 1:52:34. The 20km race went off at 12:20 p.m., and the heat and humidity were strong factors affecting everyone's times. There was no shade. The course was narrow and had tight turns at each end.

The 20km race was a good race, but there were people running as the judging was loose. The medal winners were legal walkers. Sin Nakamichi of Japan got second in the race and Jack Bray was third. Sin led for about 8km when Jack and I caught him. It went back and forth with the three of us changing positions. The last lap, I was in the lead and had slowed up a little, but Sin and Jack had slowed more. I thought I had a sufficient lead, but when I was nearing the final turn to the finish line, a Japanese man came up behind me and wanted to pass. Thinking it might be Sin, I did not let him. I also knew that I could not keep up the speed, yet I was afraid to take the time to look at his number. When I finally saw that he was in the M55 age group, I relaxed a little and he did go by me.

The Men's 5km race in Miyazaki is told through the eyes of Jack Bray who won the gold medal in an American M60 Age-Group Record time of 25:09. Max won the silver in 25:11.

Before the 5km race, the Chief Judge, an IAAF judge, came to the start line to routinely give us the rules. He said that he did not want to disqualify anybody and he told us about the Warning Board. Then he said, "When you go by and look at the board, if you don't see your number say, Thank you, God. If you see your number, say, God help me!"

In the 5km there were close to 47 racewalkers so they split us into two heats. Because Max and I were anxious to race with the Japanese gold medal winner in Turku, Sin Nakamichi, we wrote a petition requesting this and gave it to Sandy Paxton our U.S. representative. She said she would do what she could do. One hour before the race, all 47 of us were lined up at the start. We learned that Sin was in the first heat and we were in the second. Sin virtually raced by himself and lapped his field many, many times finishing in an excellent time of 25:19 which broke the old American record of 25:43.

Max and I watched him and of course knowing his finish time, we knew exactly what we had to do to win. I pulled the pole position and Max was in the fourth position on the start line. I went through the first 220 and heard breathing over my right shoulder and looked back, and it was Max. I went through the 440 at 1:55 and again Max was right behind me. At that moment I said, "Oh, my God, I'm going to have a race on my hands."

Max never let his breathing or footsteps leave my side at any time. He tried to pass me several times and I felt the push, but had made a bond with myself not to let him pass. I said to myself, "I've come all this way. I didn't get the gold in the 20km. It's my turn." When I heard the bell for the last lap, I pulled out all the stops and gave a spurt to lengthen the distance. Coming to the last 220, I kept telling myself, "I'm fine. I'm fine. I'm fine." I made the turn towards the finish line and gave it another little kick. I could see Max a little farther back. Then all of a sudden, he was right behind me as I crossed the finish line. He almost caught me at the end. I did 25:09 and Max did 25:11.

L to R: Don Johnson, Bob Mimm

Giulio De Petra

DON JOHNSON (M75)
ROBERT MIMM (M65)

I have never been one to read every running magazine and what have you. The time you spend doing that, you could be out training. Why read about someone else doing something when you can be doing it. — Mimm

Masters starting to racewalk have to be patient. I tell them, "Don't watch the fast guys. Get with your own speed group and gradually improve. If you are talented enough you will naturally move right up." — Johnson

I Racing & Training
New Racewalkers
Competitive Spirit
Nutrition

THE REMARKABLE JOHNSON AND MIMM

On March 7, 1993 Don Johnson age 76 and Robert Mimm age 68 competed in the Los Angeles Marathon with the temperature over 90 degrees. Less than two weeks later on March 19, 1993 they competed in the 3000m race on an indoor track at the Masters Indoor T&F Championships in Bozeman, Montana, elevation 4,755 feet and temperature 74 degrees. Don did a gold medal performance in both events, finishing the Marathon in 6:34:14 and the 3000m race in 21:58.0. This is especially remarkable as Don was battling prostate cancer and died in 1994.

Proving himself to be one of America's most formidable walkers, Bob Mimm finished the L.A. Marathon second overall in a time of 4:47:54. He then turned around to win a gold at the Masters Indoor Championships with a 3000m time of 17:18.7. Bob started racewalking in 1955 and was 23rd in the Rome Olympics. He has won innumerable national and international championships since. In July 1995, he won golds in the 5km, 30:08, and 20km, 2:11:44, at the National Masters Outdoor Championship in East Lansing. He won the gold in the 20km, 2:10:12, and the silver in the 5km, 29:44, at the WAVA Games in Buffalo.

The following is taken from an interview with Don and Bob held at the Outdoor Nationals in Spokane, Washington in 1993.

RACING & TRAINING

How were you both able to combine long and short distance training to do so well at the L.A. Marathon and the Masters Indoor Nationals?

DON: I could combine the two because I am not racing at my peak and my times are not that great. I am just trying to stay with racewalking and am not training that intensely. For me, the Marathon and the 3000-meter race were just two walks. It was a matter of just going out and doing them, especially in Los Angeles. I have a swollen leg and interestingly the Marathon actually helped it. It was less swollen when I got through.

At the Indoor race, there were quite a few complaints about the altitude and dry heat in the arena, but I was not walking fast enough to really notice them. I could see that some of the other walkers were having quite a bit of trouble, especially with the altitude.

In Los Angeles, on the other hand, I was so worried about finishing the Marathon that I did not worry about the heat. Again, I was not going fast enough to have it really bother me. However, I did come home sunburned.

BOB: People ask me about my training methods expecting some real secrets, but I really do not have any. I like variety and do a lot of different workouts. I do not really follow any program. Training is just something you have to do without thinking. I am not a morning person. I like to train in the afternoon or evening.

The last few months, my son Clifford has been training with me which has helped. I trained for the L.A. Marathon with him. We went to a hilly park and did at least two hours of walking there on the weekends. That training was enough to get me through the Marathon. I have never really considered myself a long distance person. It is a chore for me to do a marathon or 50km, and the first couple of hours afterwards I really hurt. However, I usually recuperate fairly quickly.

Did you do any speed training for the Indoor 3000?

BOB: That is my problem. I am not doing enough speed work and I guess that is why my times are not that fast any more. What you hate doing the most is what you need the most. I think a competitor needs speed work, but I have been doing many garbage miles. At my age that might not be all bad because it minimizes the risk of injury.

I never used to have leg problems. Now, preventing injury is a concern as I had a lot of injuries a few years ago. When I was younger, I did not get injured, but as you get older, the tendons tighten up. Besides, I do not stretch as much as I should. I only stretch when I happen to think about it.

Don, how is your health affecting your walking?

DON: If I go by the blood tests, I should be okay. You can never say for certain with prostate cancer. I had chemotherapy and am on negative steroids. These treatments have had their effects and it is not so easy coming back at 76. I can talk myself out of training now, and it shows in my times. In Turku (1991), I walked a 20km in 2:10 and in Spokane (1992), I walked a 20km in 2:27.

There is no real serious pushing now. It used to be the other way around. Everything else had to wait until the training was over. I always used to train longer than the distance I was racing. If I was training for a 20km, I made sure that I could go 30km.

When I first started walking, I was amazed when I went three miles and then five miles. The first thing I knew I was training for 50km's. I did a lot of 50km's the first six ye ars. Now I find that I am strong enough, but not fast.

When did you start walking?

DON: I had my first race just before I turned 50, so I have been racing about 26 years now. I used to train all year long at least five days a week. This meant training inside during the really bad weather. I would pick a race to do about five weeks ahead as a goal for my training. The next four weeks I would do a lot of little races, often being beaten. Then, when the big race came, I would blow everyone's minds. They would say, "What happened to you?" I would reply, "Nothing. This is the race I wanted to walk."

I do ten minutes of stretching when I get up in the morning, but I should do 30 minutes. I am lazy. If I do not warm up at all, I cannot race. I am a great complainer if they start a race early and I have not had a chance to warm up. The shorter the distance, the more you need to warm up.

NEW RACEWALKERS

How would you advise masters coming into the program?

BOB: I think is important to tell masters who are beginning to racewalk in their 50s and 60s that racewalking is not easy. Many people think racewalking is much easier than running. When they find out that it is not so easy, they lose interest. Let them know how it really is before they start. Also, let them know a good coach is of tremendous value, though I think the coach's primary task is providing motivation.

DON: Elite masters runners will say in a semi-serious way, "When we have trouble running maybe we will switch over to racewalking." I always reply, "If you are thinking of racewalking, I suggest that you get started because you are going to find that it is not as easy as you think."

Some runners take to it right away, but some never really get the hang of it. If these runners had switched over earlier, they could have competed as racewalkers for the rest of their lives. As it is when they are through running, they are through competing.

BOB: When they televise the marathon at the Olympics, the announcers keep saying how tough it is, how grueling, and how it is the most difficult event in the Olympics. They never think of the 50km walk which is much more difficult than the marathon. Believe me. I have done both. Running a marathon is easy compared to 31 miles of racewalking.

DON: Masters starting to racewalk have to be patient. I tell them "Don't watch the fast guys. Get with your own speed group and gradually improve. If you are talented enough you will naturally move right up." I also tell them not to be afraid of distance, and that once they are in condition, they will feel they can go forever.

THE COMPETITIVE SPIRIT

How would you define the competitive spirit?

DON: The competitive spirit is individual to each person. Some competitors have to go by the book and do all the advised training mileage. Then, when they get into a race, all they can do is what they have put in. Work in equals work out. Other people will just come alive in a race and go way beyond their training. They essentially get more out than they put in. I think the competitive spirit is something inside.

BOB: If I go into a race, I like to win. Yet if I don't win, I am ready for the next race. I know some people who will not enter a race if they do not think they can win. I think the competitive spirit is simply the desire to compete. As a competitor, I enjoy keeping up on others' records. They can be a motivating force.

NUTRITION

From an interview of Alan Wood with Bob Mimm dated April, 1993 published in the "Masters Walker."

Bob, do you have any special way of eating?

My diet is not as good as it should be, particularly in sugar and fat. I enjoy eating and go to many "all you can eat" buffets. Of course, with my activity level, I do not need to be concerned with weight gain. There are very few foods that I do not eat. I do not use health foods. I think most of them are much too expensive in relation to their actual value. I do read labels very carefully, however. I try to stay away from chemical additives, preservatives and food colorings. I do not buy Campbell's soups, for example, because they are loaded with monosodium glutamate (MSG). MSG creates a burning sensation in my stomach. I use milk in my coffee, not a packet of chemicals. I may have used more alcohol than I should have in the past, but I enjoy wine and find meals more enjoyable with it. Besides, wine keeps me from eating too fast.

GIULIO DE PETRA (M80)
70 YEARS OF RACEWALKING

If I miss a day of training, I feel guilty. My body does not feel good. So every morning I am out as soon as it is light and the time I spend walking sets me up for the rest of the day.

PROFILE

Giulio de Petra was born in Italy on December 7, 1910 and started racewalking in 1925 at age 14. His first victory was in April, 1925 at a race in Naples. In 1926, he finished second in his first Marathon Racewalking Championship. In 1927, he finished ahead of the best Italian walkers at the 20km Grand Prix of Padova. Soon afterward, he won the 25km Italian National Championship on a track and qualified for the Molinary Trophy in London, England where he represented Italy. From 1927 to the beginning of the Second World War, he continuously competed in all the national and international events. During this time, he completed his studies as a law student, earned a doctorate degree in jurisprudence and another in the social and political sciences. He also was in charge of organizing track and field in the cities of Naples, Pescara, Reggio Emilia and Pisa. His hope of competing in the 1936 Olympics in Berlin was ended when he was drafted into the Italian army and sent to Ethiopia. He emigrated to the United States in 1948 at age 37. In 1951 he moved to Carmel. His racewalking story provides an interesting retrospective on our sport.

RACEWALKING IN ITALY 1920-1936

Italy had a very, very good group of racewalkers in the 1920s. My inspiration was Ugo Frigerio who won the men's 3km and 10km walks at the 1920 Olympics in Antwerp, Belgium, and the men's 10km in the 1924

Olympics in Paris, France.

From the time I started racewalking my goal was to compete in the Olympics. As part of my training, I competed throughout Italy and Europe in races ranging from 3km to 25km. As it is today, the 20km was probably the most popular race.

All the major Italian cities had races, and as there were very few cars, there was no worry about traffic in the streets. The usual number of competitors in a race was between 20-40, but in the most important races such as the Tour of Naples, the Tour of Milan or the Tour of Rome, there would be 100 athletes or more. These races were called "tours" because their courses went around and through the cities.

In Italy, racewalking started in the north and spread to the south where I lived. When I started competing, a strong rivalry existed between northern Italy and southern Italy. Frigerio came from the north. There were many more walkers, not quite at Frigerio's level, but very close, and the competition was good.

Life, of course, was very different without cars for transportation. I lived in Naples and attended school on Saturdays. Almost every other Sunday, I was racing somewhere. To go from Naples to Milan, for example, was a distance of about 700km. I would get on a train Saturday evening and travel all night. My family did not have much money so I went third class and slept on wood all- night. When I arrived in the morning, I would take a shower and go to the race. After the race, I had something to eat, took an all night train back to Naples, and was ready to go to school the next morning. It was a different world then with different expectations.

I was nearing the top of my abilities in 1928 and would have been in the 1928 Olympics if the 3km and 10km walks had not been cancelled. The consensus was that these walks were too short, that the athletes could go too fast and could, therefore, loose contact with thc ground. You hear the same concerns today. When the racewalk was reinstated in the Olympics, it was at the longer 50km distance.

Competition was good in Europe in the 1930s. England, the fatherland of racewalking, had the most races. There were many important races. The 125km race from London to Brighton and back was one of the most famous. Germany, France and Spain were active in racewalking, and just before the start of WWII, Sweden, Switzerland and Lithuania began competing.

The judging was severe, especially in England. In England, judges did not give any warnings, and one judge could immediately disqualify a walker. It was a disgrace to be disqualified. It was taken very seriously. A walker lost face. Quite different from today where walkers deliberately risk breaking the rules because it takes three judges to disqualify them. Now, it is considered good race strategy to see what you can get away with without being caught.

I was training hard for the 50km walk in the 1936 Berlin Olympics. At that time, I was an outstanding 25km walker, but after 25km, I "hit the wall". I ran out of fuel and did not know what to do. I did not drink water because I thought it would slow me down if I did. I felt I needed to eat something, but did not know what to eat. The fact was at 25km I was dehydrated and out of energy.

Someone told me it would be good to eat zabaglione with coffee. I thought the eggs and sugar in zabaglione would give me energy; however, immediately after eating it, I vomited and my body felt completely dead. I was beginning to think that maybe 25km was my limit.

In 1934, I was invited to compete in the Canadian National 50km Championship near Lake Ontario. The outstanding Canadian was a man by the name of Hank Cieman. He was very tall and held the 1-mile world record. At the 25km mark, I was way ahead of everyone, but again I lost my energy. Cieman passed me and got a five or six-minute lead.

The race finished in a hippodrome, and we had to do three 1-mile loops. When I dragged myself into the stadium, a large number of Italians were there with a band playing. Somebody gave me some beautiful grapes to eat and my energy immediately came back. I could see Cieman a half mile ahead with a little over a mile left. I had regained so much energy from the grapes that I finished only 300 meters behind him. If I had one more lap, I would have won.

If only someone had told me what to eat and what not to eat, what to drink and what not to drink. But this type of information was not available as it is today.

AMERICA

It was very hard to find anyone who knew anything about racewalking when I came to America in 1948. When I eventually settled in Carmel in 1951, I became very busy teaching Italian and writing text books for the Army Language School there. I did not think any more of racewalking.

One day in 1978 I discovered I was getting a little heavy, so I thought, "What can I do?" Racewalking seemed the natural answer, and I knew it would be good for me. However, no one on the Monterey Peninsula had ever heard of racewalking. Some friends suggested that I look into teaching racewalking at the Monterey Peninsula College. Gradually, I organized a group and founded the Monterey Peninsula Walk, Walk, Walk Club in 1980.

I did not know anything about masters competition. I thought a good way to get involved in racewalking was to become a judge. I wrote Larry Larsen who sent me a test. I passed it and became a national judge. Then I had to find a race to judge. Larry gave me the name of someone in San Jose who told me about upcoming races. After that, I went to the 50km Championship at MT SAC in Southern California, and met the gang from Los Angeles - John Kelly, Jim Hanley, and Dean Ingrams as well as Frank Alongi from Michigan. They told me about masters competitions.

In Europe, masters are called veterans. I think the European program may have started after ours because at the time I was in Europe, a masters program did not exist. I have participated in almost all American and European masters national and international championships including every World Veterans Games since 1980.

Without counting team medals from the World Veterans Games, I won two silver medals in Puerto Rico (1983), two silver medals in Rome, Italy (1985), two bronze medals in Melbourne, Australia (1987), two silvers in Eugene, Oregon (1989), one gold in Turku, Finland (1991) and two golds in Miyazaki, Japan (1993). I also won four gold and four silver medals in the European Veterans Championships in Sweden, Hungary and Norway.

WALK FOR LIFE

Walk For Life would be a good title for my racewalking biography. This is exactly what I am doing and I really believe in it. If I miss a day of training, I feel guilty. My body does not feel good. So every morning I am out as soon as it is light, and the time I spend walking sets me up for the rest of the day. It is a very healthy sport and a very important part of my life.

My present goals depend on my health. I would like to racewalk until the day before I die. I do not have time goals now. As the years go by, my speed slows. It is something that bothers me because I feel young. I do not feel the years. I feel as young inside as I did at 50. And so I say, "Why do I go so slow?" I used to walk a 5km in 23+ minutes or a 10km in 47+ minutes, and a 20km in 90+ minutes. Now I walk a 5km in 36+ minutes, a 10km in 70+ minutes, and a 20km in 2 hours and 30 minutes.

There is not too much difference in the workouts I did when I was in my 70s and those I am doing now in my 80s. The major change is in the number of days I train. I used to train almost every day and rarely took a day off. Now I rest one day, and if necessary two days, every week. In addition to walking, I go to a fitness center for stretching and exercise very lightly on a few machines. During my workouts, I always concentrate on the real walking technique and never run to improve my walking speed.

Racewalking as it is practiced today is a new sport. It does not resemble the pure style of racewalking I love. The quest for speed has blurred the line between walking and running.

CHAMPIONSHIPS, AWARDS, RECORDS AND GOVERNING BODIES

BEV LaVACK

BOB FINE

BEV LA VECK

I Age-Graded Tables & Age-Factors
II USATF 5-Year Age-Group Records
Road Records and Track Records
Rules
Regional Championships
III Annual Racewalking Awards -
Increase in Masters Racewalkers
IV World "Best Times"
World Age-Group Performances

AGE-GRADED TABLES & AGE-FACTORS

Bev discusses the development of the Age-Graded Tables and Factors for racewalking published by "National Masters News". ***Age-Graded Tables:*** *These tables serve as a common denominator for comparing the scoring of an 80-year-old and a 40-year-old. They work well when you want to score men and women in a race together or separately, or when you want to compare performances in several events (such as at a track and field meet).* ***Age-Factors:*** *Factors can be used to compare an individual's performance in a given event with what he/she did, or might have done in his/her prime. The factor expresses the rate of decline based on Age. It converts a performance to the equivalent performance of an open-class athlete.*

In 1994, World Amateur Veterans Association (WAVA) approved new Age-Graded Tables for all track and field events. It was a real challenge to come up with a system that is fair and approximately equal across events and ages so that you can compare racewalkers to runners, for example. Al Sheahen and Rex Harvey put a tremendous amount of time into this. (Al is the Editor of "National Masters News" and Rex is the USATF Masters Multi-Events Coordinator. Both are members of the WAVA Council.)

The World Single-Age Bests were useful in making "reality checks" of the racewalk tables. Without them, there was a danger of making the tables so tough that nobody scores over 85 percent, or so easy that walkers score over 100 percent. I do not know how we could have done this without an active list of men's and women's performances by single age.

When it is understood that Single-Age Bests have no status as records, they can be useful. The only official records are the 5-Year Age-Group Records ratified by USATF. However, Single-Age Bests furnish very exciting data. They offer a way of finding out what people can do and what is realistic to expect at specific ages.

Single-Age Bests also provide a "history" of racewalkers who have been competing for many years. Racewalkers show tremendous swings in their times over a decade. For one or two years, they will walk relatively slowly. Then they will have a few years of very fast performances only to slow down again. Motivation, time, health, and other activities all enter into their race times. You do not see the steady decline that you might associate with aging.

It was a challenge accommodating the stellar performances in the new Age-Graded Tables. I feel that exceptional performances cannot be considered flukes. I think they do set a standard. Therefore, in computing the tables, I used the times of the best men and women performers, their Single Age Bests, and tested these bests with the proposed Age-Graded Tables to see how close to 100 percent they would come. When we came up with scores over 100, we would change the tables to accommodate the stellar performer.

We discovered some amazing performances by such standouts as Great Britain's James Grimwade (in his 70s) and Sweden's Brita Tibbling (in her 60s and 70s). To my knowledge we failed to accommodate only one extraordinary performance. The Tables were finished when we heard of an incredible 20km time by New Zealand's Gary Little (M50), which turned out to be slightly better than a "perfect 100%."

The Tables are "anchored" by established IAAF Records at various distances. They are derived by multiplying World Record times by descending fractions or "factors." As either masters performances or world records change, the Tables become dated. Already the world record for the Men's 20km has been broken. Therefore, although the men may not realize it when they look at the Tables, they have a "gift" of a few seconds in the 20km!

AGE FACTORS

Another interesting problem Al, Rex and I had was deciding what to do about the age factors comparing men and women. At first we were going to use the same factors for both sexes. We did not know of any reason why men and women would age differently. However, when we looked at the data, the women had much lower age-graded scores. This outcome suggested that women age faster than men. The only exceptions we found were a few women runners in their 40s such as Prisilla Welch and Evy Palm. The levels of their performances did not show any decline.

Because of the overwhelming evidence that women racewalkers scored lower than men using the same factors, we began looking at the variables. For instance, in racewalking the total number of racewalkers is not that large. This is especially true of the number of women worldwide. In comparison to men, women racewalkers do not have the depth or range in ability that includes very high performers.

It is only recently that women have been accepted into the Olympics and other international competitions. Former Olympians make up a sizeable proportion of the men's fields at the World Veterans Games. There are less than a handful of comparable masters women racewalkers competing.

In the 1989 Age-Graded Tables, Al and Rex gave a 10 percent break to the women straight across the board. In 1994, we decided to give the same 10 percent break to the women because of their lower age-graded scores. This adjustment produced softer standards for women relative to the men.

I have been mulling over the real possibility that there is a difference in the aging processes of men and women and that the difference in age-graded scoring is not just caused by small sample size. At age 50, women may really start losing muscle strength at a different rate than men, even though they lift weights and do other types of muscle building activities. I now suspect that women cannot sustain the same hard training that men can. This possibility would account for the differences in their comparative times in events that require strength.

These thoughts have lead me to rationalize and to accept using different factors for men and women. We can say that theoretically men and women's factors ought to be the same, but you have to look at the data. The data says that the women are slowing down faster than the men, starting in their late 40s and early 50s. You just cannot ignore the findings to date.

This conclusion may be challenged as women Olympians join the ranks of masters. If our sport develops stronger women athletes in their 20s and 30s and if they continue to compete at high levels into their late 40s and 50s, the data may change. Like a few women runners today, the performance levels of some women racewalkers may not decline in their 40s.

REQUIREMENTS FOR OFFICIAL USATF 5-YEAR RECORDS.

ROAD RECORDS

The only way a road record of any kind (running or racewalking) can ever be ratified (recognized or made official) by USA Track & Field is if it is set on a course that conforms to the standards and procedures set up by the Road Running Technical Committee (RRTC). USA Track & Field gives the RRTC responsibility for setting course certification standards and race procedures. Marks set in events which do not conform to USATF requirements simply will not count. This is true for all age groups. Masters racewalking cannot have independent standards and policies and expect to have record times ratified by USATF. Those applying for records, for themselves or for others, should be familiar with the current *USATF Rules of Competition Book*.

The RRTC publishes lists of courses and their certification numbers by state and distance. These lists include certified racewalking courses which are short loops or out-and-back courses. Racewalkers who have the primary intent of setting a record at a specific race would be wise to check on the course certification number before they pay for their plane ticket. They would also be wise to determine that the proper number of officials will be present for timing, judging and lap counting.

TRACK RECORDS

There are firm USATF rules that cover track records. Indoors, the track must have cones if there is no inner curb, and be no longer than 220 yards. Outdoors, there must be a raised inner curb. The event must be for racewalkers only. No runners. There must be a minimum of four certified judges, at least half of whom have national certification or higher. At least one must be Master or IAAF-certified.

When an athlete sets what appears to be a new 5-year Age- Group Record, he or she should submit the official documentation. Again, the potential record-setter must use some caution in deciding where to go to set records.

When USATF started ratifying masters records in 1992, many fine times were not ratified because they were set on uncertified courses. It came as a shock to many athletes to have times tossed out that they would never equal again. It came as a shock to race directors to learn that their courses failed to meet USATF standards. Today, there are many official records on the books that are minutes slower than the "best performances" compiled by Lori Maynard, Don Henry and Alan Wood over the years.

The USATF Racewalk Committee has a person in charge of senior racewalk records, while Masters T&F has someone responsible for masters racewalk records. The same ratification requirements apply to seniors and masters, and both groups often make road records in the same events.

RECORDS

1. Masters records may be made in mixed age and/or sex competitions.
2. There may be both 5km track & 5km road race championships.
3. The hour racewalk has been added to the USATF Masters Racewalk Records since it is a USATF Championship distance.
4. The USATF Rules governing records now requires a minimum of four certified judges for a track record and six for a road course, and that at least one-half of the certified judges be certified at the national level or higher, and that at least one has Master or IAAF level certification. If a Regional Championship cannot supply this kind of judging panel, the athletes should be informed in advance. It is recommended that the quantity and level of judging be specified on entry forms along with the course certification number. All competitive racewalks require a minimum of three USATF certified racewalk judges.

CHAMPIONSHIPS

All masters racewalking falls under the jurisdiction of the Masters Track and Field Committee. Masters racewalking championship regions must correspond to those of Masters Track and Field. There are seven masters championship regions in contrast to the four regions of the USATF Racewalk Committee. (*USATF Racewalking Committee is primarily responsible for senior (or open division) athletes as well as youth, emerging elite athletes and members of the national racewalking teams.)*

Regional championships under the governance of the USATF Racewalking Committee can have masters divisions, but they are not officially masters championships unless they are separately titled according to the regions of the Masters T&F Committee given below. For example, if you live in New York and wanted to include a masters regional 10km championship along with a 10km national championship awarded by the USATF Racewalking Committee, your entry flyer would read: USATF National 10km Championship and USATF Masters Eastern 10km Championship. You would want to check with the Eastern Coordinator to make sure there was not another Regional Masters Eastern 10km Championship.

In addition to the racewalk championships held at the USATF Masters T&F Championship Meets, the following championships may (do not have to) be held: 5km road, 15km, 25km, 30km, 40km, 50km, 100km, 100 miles, 1-hour, Men's 10km and Women's 20km. A cooperative effort between the Racewalking Committee and Masters T&F has resulted in masters championships being awarded jointly with the senior racewalk championships. Bids for these championships are evaluated in the Racewalking Committee's Site Selection Subcommittee, which then recommends to Masters T&F that a National Road Walk Championship be—or not be—held.

SEVEN REGIONS OF MASTERS T&F CHAMPIONSHIPS

EASTERN: Associations: Maine, New England, Adirondack, Connecticut, Metropolitan, Mid-Atlantic, Three Rivers, New Jersey, Niagara and Potomac Valley.

SOUTHEASTERN: Associations: N. & S. Carolina, Georgia, Florida, Alabama, Virginia and Tennessee.

MIDWESTERN: Associations: Michigan, Lake Erie, Ohio, Kentucky, West Virginia, Illinois, Indiana, and Wisconsin.

MID-AMERICAN: Associations: Ozark, Missouri Valley, Nebraska, Minnesota, Iowa, Dakotas, New Mexico and Colorado.
SOUTHWESTERN: Associations: Southern, Border, Gulf, Southwestern South Texas, Arkansas, Oklahoma, and West Texas
WESTERN: Associations: Arizona, Pacific, Central, Southern California, San Diego-Imperial, Nevada and Hawaii
NORTHWESTERN: Associations: Montana, Wyoming, Snake River, Inland Northwest, Oregon, Utah, Pacific Northwest and Alaska.

FOUR REGIONS OF THE RACEWALK COMMITTEE CHAMPIONSHIPS

EAST: Associations: Maine, New England, Adirondack, Connecticut, Metropolitan, Mid-Atlantic, Three Rivers, New Jersey, Niagara, Virginia, and Potomac Valley.
NORTH: Associations: Michigan, Lake Erie, Ohio, Kentucky, West Virginia, Illinois, Indiana, Minnesota, Nebraska, Iowa, Dakotas, Wisconsin, Missouri Valley and Ozark.
SOUTH: Florida, Southern, Alabama, Tennessee, Gulf, Southwestern, South Texas, West Texas, North Carolina, South Carolina, Georgia, Oklahoma, and Arkansas.
WEST: Utah, Colorado, New Mexico, Arizona, Border, Montana, Wyoming, Snake River, Inland Northwest, Oregon, Pacific Northwest, Alaska, Pacific, Central California, Southern California, San Diego-Imperial, Nevada and Hawaii.

- Masters T&F Regional Coordinators are responsible for Masters Regional Championships.
- The 5000 meter track event usually takes place in the Masters Regional T&F meets where it should remain the responsibility of the meet organization.
- Other racewalking masters championships are not mandatory.
- Race Directors wishing to conduct a masters regional racewalk championship must clear with the Masters Regional Coordinator to avoid duplication of championship distances.

ANNUAL RACEWALKING AWARDS

Each year Bev submits names of men and women in each 5-year age-group for award consideration. The awards are presented every year at the USATF National Convention. The following explains how the winners are selected.

A few years ago, I came up with a point system for assigning awards. I did not find it completely satisfactory, however. I felt even with a point system, especially if any kind of weighting is used, subjective judgments had to be made. For example, problems arose about how many points to give a national championship versus a 5-Year Age-Group Record versus a Single-Age Best.

Some people did not want the awards automatically to go to the fastest person and felt that there were other criteria that made a racewalker outstanding. Other people wanted a very objective standard based on times alone. With the differences in opinion, I decided to switch over to a vote method which is what we are using today.

I contacted eighteen racewalkers in different parts of the country who went to a lot of meets or who were involved with many masters racewalkers. I asked them to form an advisory panel and, among other things, to vote annually for the outstanding male and female walker in each age division as well as for the overall outstanding male and female racewalker. The panel has been expanded to thirty-two members.

Every year, I supply the data the panel uses for voting. I strongly encourage masters to send me race results when they medal in championship events or when they break age-group or single-age records. This way they can be certain of being considered for the annual awards.

INCREASE IN MASTERS RACEWALKING

A quick scan of past issues of "National Masters News" provides ample evidence of the growth of masters racewalking in the past ten years, largely attributable to the huge increase in women's competition. The 1982, 1987, 1992 and 1994 USATF Tables are based on National Masters Outdoor Championships. The 1989 and 1995 WAVA Tables are based on Eugene and Buffalo. The 1995 WAVA Table refers to registered athletes. The other Tables refer to actual participants.

1982 USATF		
450 Entrants in Meet		
5km	RW	5F
5km	RW	14M
20km	RW	2F
20km	RW	11M

1987 USATF		
976 Entrants in Meet		
5km	RW	27F
5km	RW	54M
20km	RW	16F
20km	RW	40M

1992 USATF		
1075 Entrants in Meet		
5km	RW	65F
5km	RW	53M
10km	RW	49F
20km	RW	39M

1994 USATF		
1418 Entrants in Meet		
5km	RW	81F
5km	RW	85M
10km	RW	67F
20km	RW	63M

1989 WAVA		
4951 In Meet		
5km	RW	130F
5km	RW	199M
10km	RW	126F
20km	RW	179M

1995 WAVA		
5529 In Meet		
5km	RW	213F
5km	RW	327M
10km	RW	181F
20km	RW	291M

WORLD "BEST TIMES"

To call masters **world marks** "records" or "best times" is still a matter of debate. The problem with calling them records is that there is so much variation in different countries regarding course certification, judging, timing, etc. Some countries have very tight standards for records, and their record-keepers are accustomed to providing ample documentation. In other countries there is no system for evaluating and recognizing "Veterans" marks.

For example, Britta Tibbling's name is listed in the 5000 meter racewalk results of the 1989 Masters Outdoor Championships held in San Diego with a time of 29:16. However, no times from that meet are acceptable at U.S. Records because there was no continuous curb on the track. I was also present when she racewalked a 30:30 5km in Sweden in 1989 and in that race there again was no curb. In addition, the track was less than 400 meters and we had to walk approximately 13 laps.

Verification of international results at best is always difficult. U.S. Records have still not accepted racewalk marks from the 1991 World Veterans Games in Turku, Finland because of problems with verification (documentation of times, judges signatures, cubing on track, etc.) I hate to have a system for ratifying World Records which only three or four countries can meet. Because of possible deficiencies, I would personally like to see international marks clearly identified as "Noteworthy Performance" or "Bests."

The other issue of debate is whether these times (whatever we call them) should be limited to track events. Again, I would hate to have to verify course distances, and even less to verify the adequacy of judging. For example, the 1987 WAVA road walks in Melbourne were on a huge, gorgeously scenic, point-to-point course that resembled a road running course. Meet management used a large number of judges along the course so the course was probably judged more closely than most road races. Nonetheless, records set on this course did not meet official U.S. road standards for records.

WORLD AGE-GROUP BEST PERFORMANCES

July 31, 1995

event	age	time	name	year	home
3000m	M40	11:28:21	SAWALL		AUS
3000m	45	12:37.1	LANKINEN		
3000m	M50	12:34.9i	DENOON	02-94	USA
3000m	M55	13:21.2	NOKELA		FIN
3000m	M60	14:37.0	CHAPLIN		GBR
3000m	M65	15:58.3	COLMAN	07-88	GBR
3000m	M70	16:58.73	COLMAN	06-91	GBR
3000m	M75	16:19.5	GRIMWADE	12-87	GBR
3000m	M80	20:39.0	STRANG		FIN

event	age	time	name	year	home
5000m	M40	20:13.0	BALEK		YUG
5000m	M45	20:54.4	LITTLE	12-91	NZL
5000m	M50	21:01	LITTLE	02-92	NZL
5000m	M55	22:44.5	GOLUBNICH	07-91	USR
5000m	M60	24:48	HAWKINS	05-88	GBR
5000m	M65	25:44.0	DAINTRY	03-78	AUS
5000m	M70	26:29.38	DAINTRY	04-79	AUS
5000m	M75	27:40	GRIMWADE	06-87	GBR
5000m	M80	29:24.1	GRIMWADE		GBR
5000m	M85	33:15.0	THEOBALD	04-82	AUS
5000m	M90	35:18.54	THEOBALD	12-87	AUS

WORLD AGE-GROUP BEST PERFORMANCES
July 1995

event	age	time	name	year	home
10km	M40	40:39	JOBIN	07-83	CAN
10km	M45	43:44	LITTLE	10-91	NZL
10km	M50	42:20	LITTLE	02-92	NZL
10km	M55	47:56	NOKELA		FIN
10km	M60	47:48	BOMBA	09-84	ITA
10km	M65	55:24	JONES		AUS
10km	M70	54:17	DAINTRY	05-81	AUS
10km	M75	55:01	GRIMWADE	09-87	GBR
10km	M80	61:25.4	GRIMWADE	08-93	GBR
10km	M85	82:44	CONWAY	07-90	USA

event	age	time	name	year	home
20km	M40	1:21:36	SAWALL	07-82	AUS
20km	M45	1:25:03	SAWALL	04-83	AUS
20km	M50	1:26:32	LITTLE	02-92	NZL
20km	M55	1:37:04	WEIDNER	04-83	GBR
20km	M60	1:43:50	BOMBA	06-85	ITA
20km	M65	1:51:18	DAINTRY	01-81	AUS
20km	M70	1:58:10	GRIMWADE	08-86	GBR
20km	M75	1:56:19	GRIMWADE	11-87	GBR
20km	M80	2:04:49	GRIMWADE	06-92	GBR
20km	M85	2:26:07	THEOBALD	08-82	AUS
20km	M90	2:34:01	THEOBALD	04-87	AUS

WORLD AGE-GROUP BEST PERFORMANCES July 1995

event	age	time	name	year	home
50km	M40	3:49:06	J. MARIN	03-92	ESP
50km	M45	3:59:48	SAWALL		AUS
50km	M50	4:14:37	WEIDNER	08-83	GER
50km	M55	4:29:47	WEIDNER		GER
50km	M60	4:59:58	GOULD	11-77	CAN
50km	M65	5:32:55	L. CREO	04-90	GBR
50km	M70	5:33:21	COLMAN	05-91	GBR
50km	M75	5:19:34	GRIMWADE	08-87	GBR

event	age	time	name	year	home
3000m	F35	13:11.76i	HERAZO	03-95	USA
3000m	F40	13:19.7	GRIESBACH		FRA
3000m	F45	14:26.2	HEIKKILA		FIN
3000m	F50	15:11.9	HEIKKILA		FIN
3000m	F55	16:31.0	WORTH	06-88	GBR
3000m	F60	16:28.5	WORTH	07-89	GBR
3000m	F65	17:08.32	TIBBLING		SWE
3000m	F70	18:05	TIBBLING	07-89	SWE
3000m	F75	21:23.57	FORBES		NZL
3000m	F80	24:00	JEFFREYS	11-90	AUS
3000m	F85	27:36.0	JEFFREYS	09-94	AUS

WORLD AGE-GROUP BEST PERFORMANCES July 1995

event	age	time	name	year	home
5000m	F35	22.39	HERAZO	09-94	USA
5000m	F40	22:49.4	GRIESBACH		FRA
5000m	F45	24:31.3	HEIKKILA		FIN
5000m	F50	25:20.0	HEIKKILA		FIN
5000m	F55	26:46.92	ALBURY	12-87	AUS
5000m	F60	27:04	MEYER		GER
5000m	F65	28:26.7	TIBBLING		SWE
5000m	F70	29:16	TIBBLING	08-91	SWE
5000m	F75	32:44.76	TIBBLING	10-93	SWE
5000m	F80	37:41	CLARKE	07-91	USA
5000m	F85	44:43.85	ROBARTS	07-95	USA

event	age	time	name	year	home
50km	F35	5:01:52	MILLEN	1983	GER
50km	F40	4:50:51	S. BROWN	1991	GBR
50km	F45	4:56:27	S. BROWN	09-94	GBR
50km	F50	5:37:24	HOERNECKE	04-93	ESP
50km	F55	6:50:15	PETERSON	03-89	USA
50km	F60	7:27:49	M. HENRY	02-88	USA
50km	F65	6:31:12	SCOTT	05-93	GBR

WORLD AGE-GROUP BEST PERFORMANCES July 1995

event	age	time	name	year	home
10km	F35	45.53	HERAZO	06-95	USA
10km	F40	47.07	GRIESBACH		FRA
10km	F45	51:28	HEIKKILA		FIN
10km	F45	50:58p	JOHNSON	03-95	USA
10km	F50	52:02	HEIKKILA		FIN
10km	F55	57:00	MEYER	11-87	GER
10km	F60	56:38	MEYER		GER
10km	F65	58:41	TIBBLING		SWE
10km	F70	60:18	TIBBLING		SWE
10km	F75	67:46	TIBBLING	10-93	SWE
10km	F80	78:26	LINDGREN	07-91	SWE

event	age	time	name	year	home
20km	F35	1:35:39	HERAZO	05-95	USA
20km	F40	1:42:22	McDONALD	12-93	AUS
20km	F45	1:45:25	HEIKKILA		FIN
20km	F50	1:53:39	MAEDER	05-95	SUI
20km	F55	2:00:39	RICHARDSO	09-94	USA
20km	F60	2:04:34	WORTH	04-89	GBR
20km	F65	2:12:02	MEYER	05-93	GER
20km	F70	2:52:14	CROCKER	08-84	USA
20km	F75	2:49:18	CROCKER	08-87	USA

BOB FINE

I IAAF, WAVA, USATF
International - IAAF
International & Regional - WAVA
National - USATF
II IAAF Racewalking Rules by Elaine Ward
IAAF Rules & Masters Racewalking

IAAF, WAVA, USATF

The fastest growing area in masters athletics (track & field, long distance running and racewalking) is racewalking. The largest participant event at the national masters championships are the racewalks. Unlike track and field, most of the new participants in racewalking are over fifty years of age. A large percentage are women. There are three levels of governing bodies for masters racewalking:

INTERNATIONAL - IAAF

The International Amateur Athletic Federation (IAAF) is the international governing body for the sport of athletics (track & field, long distance running and racewalking). The IAAF sets the technical rules and sanctions international championships for athletes of all ages.

INTERNATIONAL - WAVA

The World Association of Veteran Athletes (WAVA) is the international administrative body for men over 40 and women over 35. WAVA receives funding from the IAAF and administers the masters (veterans) program under the aegis of the IAAF. WAVA does not, as yet, have a formal, written agreement with the IAAF, but formal affiliation should be accomplished within the next few years. WAVA recognizes the IAAF as the governing body and all WAVA Championships are sanctioned by the IAAF.

WAVA has two racewalking divisions: Stadia & Non-Stadia. Stadia consists of all events held on the track up to 10 kilometers. Non-stadia consists of all events held on the road as well as events longer than 10 kilometers on a track. At the Stadia Championships, held in odd numbered years, there are 5-kilometer races for men and women on the track, and a women's 10- kilometer road walk and a men's 20-kilometer road walk. At the Non-Stadia Championships held in even numbered years, the distances are 20 kilometers for women and 30 kilometers for men. WAVA selects the Chief Judge for these events.

REGIONAL - WAVA

WAVA has six Regions: Europe, Africa, Asia, Oceania, South America and North America. All of these Regions host track and field championships which all include racewalks. Some of the Regions also have strictly racewalking championships. As the North American Racewalking Regional Chairman, I sanction North American Racewalking Championships at distances of 3km, 5km, 8km, 10km, 15km and 20km.

NATIONAL - USATF

United States of America Track & Field (USATF) is the national governing body for athletics. USATF is affiliated with the IAAF. Within USATF there are various standing sports committees. Racewalking has two separate committees, one for open athletes and a second for masters athletes.

(1) The USATF Racewalking Committee has jurisdiction over men and women under the age of 40, and these racewalkers compete in the Open Division. (The terms senior athletes and open athletes are often used interchangeably.)

(2) The USATF Masters Track & Field Committee has jurisdiction over men and women ages 40 and above. These racewalkers are called masters and compete in 5-year Age Groups. The Masters Track & Field Committee has a Masters Racewalking subcommittee currently chaired by Bev LaVeck. Bev serves as the masters racewalking liaison between the Racewalking Committee and the Masters Track & Field Committee.

NATIONAL CHAMPIONSHIPS

When the masters program was first given status as a separate standing sports committee approximately 25 years ago, there were not enough racewalkers in both the open and masters divisions combined to have large participation in national championships. I was the National Masters Chairman at that time. An agreement was reached whereby the Racewalking Committee in charge of open athletes would include masters age group divisions in all of their national championships except for two: (1) The Masters Indoor Championships (3km for women, 5km for men) (2) The Masters Outdoor Championships (5km track for men and women, and 20km and 10km road for men and women respectively). These two Championships are held as part of the Masters Track and Field Committee's annual championships.

Since the agreement was reached to combine open and masters racewalkers in the same championships, racewalking at the masters level has exploded, especially in the last decade. As a result, there are now more masters competing than open walkers. It has become a situation where the tail is wagging the dog. It is now feasible for the masters to host their own national championships under the auspices of the Masters Track & Field Committee at all of the standard racewalking distances.

REGIONAL CHAMPIONSHIPS

Keeping in mind that there are two separate USATF governing racewalking committees, one for open or senior athletes and one for masters athletes, there are also two separate regional systems. There are four regions under the Racewalking Committee: East, South, North and West. There are seven regions under the Masters Track and Field Committee: Eastern, Southern, Midwestern, Mid-American, Southwestern, Western and Northwestern. Generally, masters racewalking combines with the four regions of the Racewalking Committee.

USATF - ASSOCIATIONS

USATF is made up of fifty-six Associations. The majority of associations correspond to state borders. California, New York, Pennsylvania and Texas have more than one Association within their borders. A few Associations have more than one state or the parts of two states within their jurisdiction. There is a wide variance between the Associations relative to Association championships. The New England, New Jersey, Niagara, Metropolitan (New York City), Potomac Valley (Washington, D.C. area), Florida, Tennessee, Indiana, Southern California, Georgia,

Pacific and San Diego Associations are most active in hosting Association Racewalking Championships.

Many Road Running Clubs have races with racewalking divisions; many simply allow racewalkers to participate. In some areas of the country such as Colorado (Denver area), Georgia, and South Florida almost all of the road running races have racewalking divisions. The Mid-America Racewalking Series consists of over 15 separate racewalks held in conjunction with 15 running events. This series primarily serves four Associations (Illinois, Indiana, Iowa and Wisconsin).

IAAF RULE CHANGES 1995

Elaine Ward

1. Revision of IAAF Rule 191.1 on the definition of Race Walking.

New Definition of Race Walking Race Walking is a progression of steps so taken that <u>the walker makes contact with the ground, so that no visible (to the human eye) loss of contact occurs. The advancing leg must be straightened (i.e. not bent at the knee) from the moment of first contact with the ground until in the vertical upright position.</u>

Old Rule: Race Walking is a progression of steps so taken that unbroken contact with the ground is maintained.

(A) During the period of each step, the advancing foot of the walker must make contact with the ground before the rear foot leaves the ground.

(B) The supporting leg must be straightened (i.e., not bent at the knee) for at least one moment when in the vertical upright position.

Commentary: Changes in Contact Rule: The new wording now conforms to what has in fact been going on for the last many years. The judges' eyes determine illegal loss of contact. The written requirement for double contact has been removed.

Commentary: Changes in Straight Knee Rule: The knee or leg must now be straight from the moment of first contact with the ground until the leg is in the vertical upright position. There is no written requirement that initial contact must be made with the heel, only that the leg must be straight on ground contact.

2. The following are the most relevant revisions of the judges' duties for masters.

(c) In road races, depending on the size of the course, there should normally be a minimum of nine judges including the Chief Judge. In track races, there should normally be six judges including the Chief Judge.

Commentary: The above change states that there should normally be six judges including the Chief Judge. The key word here is "normally" and implies an allowance for realistic adaptation to conditions.

3. The revision of Rule 191.3 and 191.4 is as follows.

Caution Competitors must be cautioned when, by their mode of progression, they are in danger of failing to comply with Rule 191.1. They are not entitled to a second caution from the same judge for the same offense. Having cautioned a competitor, the judge must inform the Chief Judge of his action after the competition.

Warning and Disqualification

(a) Each judge's proposal for disqualification (red card) is called a warning.

(b) When in the opinion of three judges, a competitor's mode of progression fails to comply with Rule 191.1 for loss of contact or bent knee during any part of the competition, the competitor having received three warnings shall be disqualified and informed of this disqualification by the Chief Judge.

(e) A white sign with the symbol of the offense on each side must be shown to the competitor when a caution is given. A red sign symbolizes the disqualification of the competitor. The red sign may only be used by the Chief Judge.

(g) A warning posting board must be used to keep competitors informed about the number of warnings (red cards) that have been handed into the Chief Judge for each competitor.

Commentary This revision and clarification of the process of judging is a decided improvement on the former wording. Again, it defines what in fact is taking place. When a competitor receives a white paddle, he or she is being cautioned about being close to a rule infraction. When the judge writes a red card, the competitor has made a rule violation and the judge is submitting a proposal or warning for an athlete's disqualification. The warning is posted on the warning board to warn the athlete of his or her status as far as disqualification. Three warnings from three separate judges equals a disqualification. When the Chief Judge receives the three required warnings on an athlete, it is his or her responsibility to remove the athlete from competition.

Judges continue to be instructed to give cautions before giving warnings. However, a caution is not deemed mandatory. As one of the most frequent complaints from competitors is "not being cautioned and finding themselves DQ'ed," it is important for athletes to understand that cautions are effectively technique instructions. They give competitors a chance to focus, make technique adjustments and remain in the race. But such instruction is not a requirement of rule enforcement.

The IAAF's rule revisions bring to a close the 1994-5 debate on the Definition of Race Walking. The revision of the straight knee rule will be of greatest interest to masters.

RACEWALKING RULES - IAAF & WAVA

Robert Fine

On all jurisdictional levels, the racewalking rules set by the IAAF are followed. Because of age considerations, WAVA has made some modifications to the rules for masters. For example, weights are lighter in some of the throwing events and hurdle heights are lower.

Over the years, some of the older masters racewalking athletes have asked for exemption from the old straight knee rule which stated that the leg had to be straight for a moment in the support, vertical position. They argued that they were physically incapable of straightening their legs due to injury, arthritis or the general wear and tear of aging, and that they were not deliberately breaking the rule. They felt that special consideration should be made for physical disability. All of the governing bodies rejected this request.

The 1995 revision of the Straight Knee Rule by the IAAF further requires a straight leg at first heel contact and a straight leg from heel contact into the vertical, upright position. I strongly advocate following the new IAAF rule. Some masters are still competing at the open level and some open competitors will eventually compete as masters. It is important to have consistency in the rules between the two age divisions.

The new Straight Knee Rule is already being practiced by most masters racewalkers because it is good technique. To land with a bent knee and then to straighten it for the vertical, upright position leads to a loss of power and drive. It is potentially harder on the knees as well. Masters have always taken the philosophic position that we are serious athletes, that we are to be treated as serious athletes and that we do not want special considerations.

APPENDIX

The following gives information on the racewalking coaches and instructors who have participated in this book. If any of the following addresses and telephone numbers become outdated, new phone numbers and addresses can be obtained through the Foundation.

FRANK ALONGI: Frank gives regular coaching and judging clinics in Michigan and Florida as he is a snowbird, and he gives special clinics in other parts of the U.S. One of his most popular, annual 3-day clinics spans the Memorial Weekend and is hosted by the Marin Racewalkers in Northern California. Frank can be reached at: 313-277-6060 in Michigan during the warm weather months, and at 407-496-5796 in Florida during the cold weather months. For information on the Memorial Weekend clinic, call Jack Bray at 415-461-6843.

BOHDAN BULAKOWSKI: Bohdan is the racewalking coach at the Olympic Training Center in La Grange, Georgia. He gives monthly 2 1/2 day racewalking camps in La Grange for new walkers as well as experienced walkers. Camps are limited to 12 members, are reasonably priced, and assisted by members of the National Team living in La Grange. For dates and information, call Rob Cole at 706-884-7635.

DON DENOON: Don is the running coach at Southern Illinois University at Carbondale. He gives racewalking clinics in Illinois, Indiana and surrounding states. He also coaches one of the members of the Women's National Racewalking Team and is expanding his racewalking coaching. For information, call Don at 618-529-4973.

MIKE DeWITT: Mike is the racewalking coach to see in Wisconsin. He is and has been the leading coach for young American racewalkers at the University of Wisconsin at Parkside in Kenosha. He has a very active masters program and can be reached at 414-551-0142.

RAY FUNKHOUSER: Ray is shifting gears from being "just a competitor" to coaching and giving clinics. He lives in New Jersey, and has given clinics in his home state as well as in neighboring states. Ray can be contacted at 908-341-7386.

RON LAIRD: Ron lives in Ohio. Ron has extensive knowledge of the sport of racewalking. He is a four-time Olympian '60,'64,'68','76, member of the Track & Field Hall of Fame, former Olympic coach and continuing masters athlete. Ron coaches and gives clinics. For information call 216-998-1371.

DAVE McGOVERN: Dave gives regular camps and clinics throughout the year from Florida to Maine and points west. He is frequently joined by Ian Whatley and other members of the National Racewalking Team. Camps are open to new walkers as well as elite walkers. Dave can be contacted at 706-883-1409 in La Grange, GA. (See below for Dave's other racewalking resources.)

SALLY RICHARDS: Sally is located in Colorado and gives clinics locally and nationally. She will be giving several women's racewalking camps from June through September of 1996. She also is planning racewalking tours to Wales and other places in '96. For further information contact Sally at her company, WalkSport, Ltd. Phone 303-674-4428, 303-674-2144.

GWEN ROBERTSON: Gwen is a regular coach in the Seattle area. She has a full coaching program and cannot extend herself further at this time, but keep alert for the future. Ruth Eberle and Bev LaVeck attest to her abilities.

MARTIN RUDOW: Martin gives clinics throughout the United States. His 1- and 2-day clinics are frequently associated with regional and national championships. These clinics often include group sessions and private coaching. Call Martin at 206-524-6081.

ELAINE WARD: Elaine lives in Southern California. She gives clinics and does private coaching and video coaching for walkers throughout the country via the North American Racewalking Foundation. See information on the Foundation. 818-577-2264

BOOKS AND VIDEOS

DAVE McGOVERN & IAN WHATLEY: Ian Whatley is the racewalking entrepreneur of Rose & Crown Design Studio. He and Dave McGovern have made a series of videos called *"Ian and Dave's low budget videos"* — meaning they are not studio production quality. They cover mobility drills and technique with "easily understood scientific explanations." Contact Ian at 240 Donington Drive, Greenville, SC 29615; Phone 803-268-5222, Fax 803-268-0065.

MARTIN RUDOW: Martin's book *Advanced Racewalking*, is the official racewalking text of the IAAF. It provides excellent information on serious training schedules. According to Martin, his newest video, "MAXIMUM WALKING" is for fitness walkers and combines walking instruction with exercises. Information and orders: Technique Productions, 4831 N.E. 44th, Seattle, WA 98105. Phone 206-524-6081, Fax 206-527-1223.

ELAINE WARD: The video *Basics of the Technique of Racewalking* and its two companion books, *Introduction to the Technique of Racewalking* and *Mobility Exercises for Racewalking* clearly and simply present the "how to's" of racewalking using walkers of all ages and sizes. Elaine's newest book, *WALKING WISDOM FOR WOMEN, Plus+ing Your Walk for Fitness, Career and Romance* is a motivational book for women. It highlights the fitness and cosmetic benefits of the racewalking technique. A fun, easy read. *MASTERS RACEWALKING* and the above books and video are available through the North American Racewalking Foundation. See order form on page 255.

OTHER RESOURCES

JACK BRAY: Coach of the Marin Racewalkers, Jack's club has one of the most successful masters teams in the country. As a world champion, Jack combines excellent technique coaching with competitive know-how. To contact Jack call 415-461-6843.

SHIRLEY CAPPS: For information on the Pilates Machine, the Massage Roller or other exercise equipment, contact Shirley at 818-797-4459 or E-mail DVBJ 32B@prodigy.com

RICHARD CHARLES: Richard lives in Austin, Texas, where he gives classes in water aerobics. For additional information on this cross training exercise and its equipment, Richard can be contacted at Tel/Fax 512-448-0118.

BEV LA VECK & BOB FINE: If you have questions about masters championships and records or about the USATF Masters Track & Field Committee, contact Bev at Tel/Fax 206-524-4721. An active organizer and promoter of racewalking in Florida, Bob is a major source of information about the Rules and Procedures of the IAAF and WAVA. Phone 407-499-3370; Fax 407-495-5054.

AVAILABLE THROUGH FOUNDATION

Visa/Mastercard 1-800-898-5117. Information 1-818-577-2264, E-mail: NARWF@aol.com; Fax: 818-577-2264. Checks to NARF at P.O. Box 50312, Pasadena, CA 91115-0312. US CURRENCY. Californians add .0825 for state tax. Shipping $3 for 1-3 items; add .40 cents each additional item. Priority $5 for 1-3 items.

——-VIDEO & BOOKS By Elaine Ward and The Southern Cal Walkers with Frank Alongi as consultant.

$24.95 **BASICS OF RACEWALKING TECHNIQUE - VIDEO** 32 minutes. Used by instructors throughout the country.

$ 8.00 **INTRODUCTION TO RACEWALKING TECHNIQUE**

$ 8.00 **MOBILITY EXERCISES FOR RACEWALKING**

$12.95 **WALKING WISDOM FOR WOMEN** A motivational book for women highlighting the fitness and cosmetic benefits of the racewalking technique. A fun, easy read.

———MORE BOOKS

$14.95 **MASTERS RACEWALKING, 30 American Coaches and Athletes Share Ideas on Technique, Training and Racing**

$ 8.00 **YOUTH RACE WALKING MANUAL** by Eugene Dix.

$16.95 **THE VALIANT HEART** By Gordon Wallace. At age 65, Gordon had triple bypass heart surgery and became an international age-group champion. Hard cover.

$25.00 **RACE WALKING IN AMERICA, PAST AND PRESENT** By Gordon Wallace. Gordon's Doctoral Dissertation.

$10.00 **WALKING** By Casey Meyers. The best comprehensive book about walking on the market.